Quotes from
Reviews for The Zen Approach to Modern Living Vol 1

"Wisdom, insight and compassion are dominant aspects of this book - I am looking forward to reading more texts by this author!"

This is a mesmerising book that when I started to read, I felt that I could not put down… I have read quite a lot of psychology books before, but this one is quite different in its accessibility and simplicity. Gedall clearly deeply cares about his reader and offers insights and self-help tools through guiding them on a spiritual journey. This stands out to me to be an exceptionally sagacious book, written from the heart and offering people tools to deal with their lives. It is also filled with common sense strategies for developing internal coping mechanisms.

… , the author wrote this book to be informative, on the one hand. On the other, he seeks to be self-help resource. When you take into consideration that what we are provided with comes from the real world experience of the author, we can place the proper value judgement on this book.

We are given practice, not just a theory that sounds good but doesn't stand up to the rigors of the real world.

…. who was the book written for? Quite literally, everyone. For me, for you, for your friends and family, even for your enemies. Chapters deal with the topic of friends, allies, family and enemies. In the real world, there is a place for all of these people.

Understandably, the author has been thorough by addressing this wide range of topics. It is well written, informative, and will be a very positive resource to have for those people who are genuinely interested in finding a workable alternative to the everyday stressors and complications that modern living brings with it. Highly recommended for an audience ranging from 12 to 100 years of age…

"A fantastic journey through self-improvement to positively benefit you and everything around you".

It guides you through methods to positively change not only your life, but also benefit the life of those around you.

It is a win-win situation and it is not crucial what age are you - anyone can apply these principles to enjoy your life to the fullest….

… This book in itself, is a form of encouragement to help us attain some form of self-actualization by rediscovering new ways in which we build our self-esteem, learn to socialise and date other people and understand the motivational drive we need to make us live life in a meaningful way without losing our identity….

"Pearls of Wisdom"

…Low self-esteem? Wrestling with some inner demons? Conflicted, confused or frustrated with people around you—family, friends or co-workers? Or even with yourself?

Then you definitely need to read this book.

Treat yourself to a more harmonious approach to all your conflicts and find solutions with the author's pearls of wisdom and clever guidance.

Very well done. Pick up a copy now. You'll be glad you did!
Highly recommended….

"A great guide to being your best self"

The Zen Approach to Modern Living

Volume 2

Work - Paradise Or Purgatory

By

Gary Edward Gedall

Copyright © Gary Edward Gedall 2017

Published by

From Words to Worlds,

Lausanne, Switzerland

www.fromwordstoworlds.com

Images synthesized by Boris:
encrypto@hotmail.com

**Paperback / Print Edition
ISBN: 2-940535-37-8
ISBN 13: 978-2-940535-37-8**

Copyright © 2017 by Gary Edward Gedall All rights reserved.

By the same Author

The Island of Serenity, Pt 1 Destruction
(Series – published or in preproduction)

Book1 :	**The Island of Survival**
Book 2:	**Sun & Rain**
Book 3:	**The Island of Pleasure (Vol 1) Venice**
Book 4:	**The Island of Pleasure (Vol 2) Japan**
Book 5:	**Rise & Fall**
Book 6:	**The Island of Esteem (Vol 1) The Knight's Tale**
Book 7:	**The Island of Esteem (Vol 2) Le Morte d'Arthur**
Book 8:	**The Faron Show**
Book 9:	**The Island of Love**

Adventures with the Master

REMEMBER

Non Fiction

The Zen approach to Low Impact Training and Sports

The Zen approach to Modern Living

    Vol 1 Fundamentals, Family & Friends

    Vol 2. Work; Paradise or Purgatory?

    Vol 3 Life Cycle

Picturing the Mind:

Vol 1 Basic Principals

Vol 2 Fields within Fields

Vol 3 Pathology, classical, traditional and alternative healing methods

Disclaimer:

The characters and events related in my books are a synthesis of all that I have seen and done, the people that I have met and their stories.

Hence, there are events and people that have echoes with real people and real events, however no character is taken purely from any one person and is in no way intended to depict any person, living or dead.

My books are not, in themselves, therapy books and are not meant to contradict or invalidate, any other vision of the human being or their psyche, nor any particular therapy.

Introduction

(Taken from Book 1, edited for Book 2)

Dear Reader,

This book is not about the spiritual practice or philosophy of Zen.

This book is about you.

About how you are living your life; about your relationship with your work, those that you work for and those that you work with.

Of course, there are no magic formulas to life, but there some basic ideas that I have found to work quite well.

This is the third book that I have written of the series, 'The Zen Approach to …', and I have felt obliged to write it because I have started to find the concept of the Zen Approach to Modern Living, has begun to become a constant companion in my life.

However, that has not stopped my daughter from questioning the validity of my writing this book, as she finds me far from living a Zen approach to anything.

I respond that I am seeking like anyone and everyone else, and that I am also on this path.

And that, as long as I am on this path, I am seeking to understand and work on myself, and that this process can help me to have interesting things to share with others.

Not only am I often aware of this in my private life, but this concept has also become something that I am sharing more and more with my patients, and I am noticing how much sense it makes in many, many situations.

However, I am neither Moses, nor Mohammad, nor a 'pure channel', nor even a latter-day Eileen Caddy. I do not have all the answers to all of life's problems and difficulties.

This is not meant to be a new form of Bible, where you will always find the perfect response to every situation.

I have taken one simple idea, 'the Zen Approach', and have looked how this concept can be applied to many situations in daily life.

Private, professional, family, social, or any and every situation that we may find ourselves in, we can call upon this vision of ourselves and the universe.

As I have said, it is not a miracle pill, there are no miracle cures.

However, I do firmly believe that the concept has value, and that by keeping conscious of it, we can greatly improve our daily lives.

I have also chosen to add a number of allegoric tales to enrich the chapters and to facilitate the entering of the energy behind the words into the deeper parts of your consciousness's.

I feel that it is also of value to read these tales, they are not just added to 'pump up the book', they are meant as an integral part of a global, learning process.

I hope and trust that this book and the ideas behind them improve and enrich your life.

Clearly, I can only deal with a very limited number and type of relationships and people. And you might find yourself frustrated, even irritated with the examples that I give.

For this, I apologise in advance, I've done my best.

Please feel free to write to me if you have any comments or feedback, and of course, any reviews or sharing about this book would be greatly appreciated.

With my kindest regards,

Gary Edward Gedall,
Lausanne, Switzerland 16 07 2017

. gary.gedall@bluewin.ch

Contents Page

Section 1 – A general reflection on yourself and the working environment 2
1. Reminder of the basics - 3
What is the Zen Approach? 3
   1.1 Basic concepts 3
   1.2 Living with Sin 7
2 Step 1 - What do I want? 14
   2.1 Choosing a direction 14
   2.2 Short, Medium or Long Term Goals 21
   2.3 Why do I work? 25
   2.4 Predators and prey 31
3 Step 2 – Getting a job 37
   3.1 Opening up to getting a job 37
   3.2 Theo, the shipping clerk. 39
   3.3 Allied Records 44
   3.4 Reflexions on being open. 52
   3.5 Shrinking or stretching? 54
   3.6 How much are you worth? 60

3.7 Toad Transport 62
3.8 Getting in 71
3.9 Written and Unwritten Conditions .. 76
Section 2 – Your Co-workers, Bosses and Subordinates 79
General introduction to this section. 79
4. Your Co-workers 81
4.1 Colleagues – First Encounters 81
4.2 The turtle and the sloth 88
4.3 The bitch 92
4.4 Miss Vera Pitkin-Hammond 95
4.5 The lost cause 100
4..6 The fox 104
4.5 Brer Rabbit goes to work 106
4.6   The Busy Beaver, Best Boy 117
5. Your Boss 131
5.1 Some Thoughts on Evil Bosses 132
5.2 Jekyll and Hyde 134
5.3 Trumping Mr. Hyde with Dr Jekyll. 138
5.4 The Vampire 141

5.5 Staking out the Vampire 144
5.6 The Invisible Man 150
5.7　Napoleon 153
5.8 The Great and Powerful Oz 160
5.9 The Donkey and the Cock 164
5.10　The Marquis de Sade 168
5.11 Some theoretical concepts 171
5.12 Kill with a borrowed sword 181
6.　Your Subordinates 191
6.1　It's good to be king 191
6.2 Pushing and Pulling, the Carrot or the Stick 199
6.3 The Shambling Sloth 201
6.4 The Pandered Poodle 206
6.5 Dory the blue-tang flatfish 210
6.6 The Cheeky Monkey 212
7 Final Reflections 226
Other works 227

Section 1 – A general reflection on yourself and the working environment

1. Reminder of the basics - What is the Zen Approach?

[For this section, I have benefitted from reworking much of the material that I have already used for the beginning of Book 1.]

1.1 Basic concepts

The Zen approach, is based on the simple idea of being in harmony with yourself and with those others around you. (Not rocket science, is it?)

Although I use the concept of 'The Zen Approach', throughout this book and these series of books, I allow myself to use the word 'Zen', only as a popular term, meaning 'being in peace and inner harmony'.

There is no intention to lead one to enter into a serious spiritual practice. (Although that wouldn't necessarily be such a bad thing.)

The Zen Approach:

All too often we find ourselves in conflict both with others and, or, with ourselves.

It is this lack of inner harmony; creating conflicts, both within and 'with-out', that produces friction and resistance.

Friction; when trying to slide an object, causes heat and slows down movement.

Resistance; in an electric wire creates heat and dissipates the energy. The more resistance, the less ability one has to move the energy forward.

Likewise, friction and resistance in relationships either externally or internally, cause 'heat', (increasing the conflict), slow us down and waste our energy.

Another interesting image that I use is that of a rug.

If we rub the surface, going against the sense of the fibres, it feels rough and we end up pushing it into a number of folds.

The more folds that we create, the more difficult it becomes to continue to advance.

On the other hand, (no pun intended, not really), if we stroke the rug following the sense of the fibres; they are soft and smooth to the touch, and the rug stays flat on the floor, allowing for a pleasant experience.

When we 'rub someone up the wrong way', not only is it uncomfortable for all concerned, (we feel the friction), but also, we create, more and more resistance, blocking our desire to smoothly advance towards our goal.

Which, not surprisingly, tends to waste an enormous amount of energy and resources.

Hence; by being in harmony with ourselves, and those around us, we can succeed to benefit from this hither to, wasted energy. And therefore, be more active, creative and positive in our lives, and our projects.

It is finding the ways to resolve those primary conflicts and connect to a deep inner harmony that the Zen approach is based.

Unfortunately, really being in harmony with ourselves and with others is very much the exception, not the rule.[1]

---

[1] Nb. The repetition of some of the words in this and the following chapters is not at all accidental.

1.2 Living with Sin

The original and basic meaning of the term, 'sin', going back to the Hebraic root, is חָטָא, chata ('ah) to 'miss'.

As in, missing the mark or the target.

Now, what can that possibly have to do with our common understanding of the term, and what does this have to do with the Zen Approach?

Short answer; everything.

We all have, within ourselves, a set of value judgements, how we should act, talk, deal with life, be treated etc. One could term this as our ideal of ourselves, and our fundamental vision of who we are in the world.

In a similar vein, we also have the ideal of how our work environment should be; how we should deal with our careers, our bosses, our colleagues, subordinates, etc.

When things fail to be; when they fall short, when the person that we are, or others show themselves to be, the way we accept to be or are treated, is far from the 'target' of the ideals that we expect.

Then we feel bad, we feel shame, we feel angry, we feel guilty, basically, simply, we suffer.

The Zen concept is simply based on bringing our outer realities together with our own inner truths.

So, is that all there is to it? Behave in the way that we are trained to, and demand that others follow your own inner sets of values, and hence, everything will be fine?

'Fraid not, nothing is ever that easy.

It is obvious that the rest of the world is not even going to know what are your innermost, core values, never mind that they would have absolutely no intention to act on them!

'But', one might well remark, 'I can at least live my life according to my inner values.'

Excellent reflection.

Clearly, if it was that easy to live our lives according to the truths and values that we have integrated, then wouldn't we all be doing that, all the time?

So, why are we not doing so?

For the obvious reason, that it is just not possible.

Okay, so, why is it not possible?

For two reasons.

Firstly; many of these values are below the level of consciousness, so we don't even know what they are. All that we know is that we feel bad, that we or someone else, has done something 'wrong'.

And secondly; many of the values are unclear, imprecise, and realistic only in certain contexts.

Otherwise, they can be; unreasonable, contradictory, illogical, and, or based on a poor emotional education.

Here is not the place for a long discussion on how we have been created as human beings, and the weird and wonderful values and beliefs that we have been indoctrinated with.

So I will limit myself to, 'a poor emotional education'.

Many of us have grown up with certain emotional challenges; lack of confidence, poor self-images, a need to be perfect, etc. These are what I refer to as, a poor emotional education.

Taking the time and the effort to find out who we are, 'know thyself', has been a standard directive for a better life since time immemorial.

And it is equally important if you are to succeed to find a healthy and balanced life.

Once we start to become aware of who we are, what we believe and how we judge how we and others behave.

Then we can work towards:

a)   Changing our way of functioning to be more in tune with these values.
Or

b)   Questioning and hence changing these values, to more fit into our normal daily lives and interactions.
Or

c)   Allowing for the distance between the 'ideal' and the 'realistic'.

Maybe accepting that we have failed to (re)act as we realise we could have, but it's not so important, and hopefully, another time, we'll do better.

Or,

d)   Accommodating the idea, that life is imperfect, and that there are likely to be things that we do not accept, but we have to live with.

Or,

e)   Begin a process of change for one or the other, or both, of the 'ideal' and the 'realistic'. All the while choosing to direct our attention towards bringing the two together.

And yet, being rational enough, to be aware that approaching the two is a lifetime challenge, one which one is likely never to accomplish.

And still being satisfied to take this journey and living as serenely as possible with this separation.

If reminds you a little of Kipling's 'If'[2], this is also not totally by chance.

---

[2] "If—" by Rudyard Kipling, written in 1895, First published in Rewards and Fairies by Doubleday, Page & Company, 1910

The poem is, in itself, a series of emotional and personal challenges, that we could you do well to attempt to face and conquer.

Leading a happy and balanced, fulfilled and acceptable life, is also a major undertaking.

These books on the Zen Approach, are not manuals on how to lead the best life, they are more list of the tests that you will need to succeed, to reach the level where you will find that best life.

2 Step 1 - What do I want?

2.1 Choosing a direction

Before starting any journey, it is usual to ask where one is planning to go.

Our professional path is no different.

Do we want to challenge ourselves to reach a difficult, far-off destination? One that will necessitate much investment, planning and maybe a little danger?

Or a safe, easily attained objective? With only the most minimal of costs in time or energy?

Do we wish to take the fastest highways or would we prefer the scenic routes?

Would it be a path that is known to your family?

Or something virgin, new and hitherto unexplored?

Strangely enough, most of us do not take enough time to question the directions and destinations where we are heading.

We take an idea, often based on our reading of the wishes and expectations of those around us, (formally expressed or not), and blindly follow it.

From very personal experience; my parents, (especially my father) did not value higher education. My family owned shops and stores, so I chose a management degree.

Somewhere hoping that this would somehow find favour in my father's eyes.

Needless to say, it didn't, and, as for me, with my Business degree, (with honours), I have never ever had a job that was in any way linked to it!

My greatest regret in life was to have not taken the opportunity to go to cinema school and study professional writing and direction.

The Zen Approach, as I continue to repeat, is simply being in harmony with yourself and being in harmony with your environment.

Knowing who you are and what you really want is primordial to this.

We are trained, educated, indoctrinated from our most earliest years to fit into the norms and values of our; families, friends, social, religious, and even political groups.

This is how we are formed to be human beings, and it would not work otherwise.

However, from within all these wishes and expectations of all these influences, there is a unique being that emerges.

You are that unique being.

You come into this world with something of a pre-formed personality.

Having been present at the births of all my children, I can vouch for this.

I have seen them grow up and something of the character traits that expressed themselves within the first few hours of birth, are still there.

Also, the messages of who and how to be, that come from our environments are rarely all coherent with each other.

We are exposed to all sorts of life philosophies through books, films, television and radio.

And now, with the advent of the internet, we are subject to a vastly increased access to all types of attitudes and values, that we can be influenced by.

All these influences can be either explicate or implicate.

I never discussed my (first) university choices with my parents, I just 'felt' what was the right direction to go into.

Looking back, with the wisdom of the years, and thinking of how much my father loved films, maybe he would have been more in tune with me studying cinema, even if he, himself could not openly admit it.

And yet, maybe even that dream of mine is only an expression of my father's, who had to give up his dream of being a professional musician, due to a car accident.

So, it is complicated, and maybe it is not even possible to ever be totally sure what our 'real' motivations for doing something might be.

As we are only the sum of all the experiences that we have ever had, (plus a bit of predisposition), who we are, must also reflect the wishes and aspirations of those people that we have been in contact with.

What is possible, is to take the time to reflect, and to try to feel, what is right for you, at this time.

When you feel clearly what your path is, go for it.

Even if there are others, even professionals that cannot see that this is right for you.

The list of successful people that were rejected or criticised is long; from J.K. Rowling, to Fred Astaire, Sylvester Stallone, Marilyn Monroe, Walt Disney and Steven Spielberg to Steve Jobs and Albert Einstein, just to name a few.

Of course, you might make mistakes, be directed towards the wrong path, fool yourself, be fooled by others.

This is not the worst that can happen. The worst that can happen, is, if you clearly realise that this is the wrong route, to not change direction, get off of the; road, bus, train.

Find the next off-ramp, stopping place, station.

However, unless and until you find out that this is wrong for you, then keep going.

One of the most stubborn people that I know has been writing, off and on, his whole life. He has just turned 60, but has not yet found the success that he is looking for in his writing.

He has no intention of giving up his dream, and has a list of 20 more books on his 'writing list'.

I believe that he can make it.

So do you.

How do I know?

Because you are reading this book!!!

2.2 Short, Medium or Long Term Goals

This is a subject that traverses the whole of everything in your life.

How much are you willing to invest now, to reap the reward at some future date?

We are taught from the youngest age that we need to cope with the frustration of not having everything so soon as we desire it.

"No, you can't have that sweet, (candy bar), now."

"***First you***; do your homework, tidy your room, clear the table, ***then you can***; go out to play, watch TV, play with your toy."

Starting a diet, a fitness regime, or studying a new subject, all demand that with give before we get.

Even in a regular job, we need to work for a full week or month before we can expect a salary check.

However, this is nothing compared to the investment in time or energy to become a doctor or a lawyer, to name but the two most popular of these careers.

And then we should add to the reflection, the risk of not succeeding to make a career of your chosen profession.

If we move towards the more creative and artistic dimensions; actor, singer, musician, visual artist, to name the most precarious.

We know well that the chances of earning a living from one of these occupations is less than guaranteed.

This doesn't mean that you shouldn't follow your dream, that is not the point of this reflection.

We just need to consciously make the choice to follow these routes. Trusting that our desire, our passion is enough to carry us forward during the dark moments of questioning, that we all experience, at some time or other.

For instance; I have participated twice to the Geneva Book Fair and once to the London Book Festival.

Each time, about half way into the event, I question myself about the cost benefits of being there.

Fortunately, I succeed to respond to that negative reflection in that I am on a long-term project and each of these investments is taking me forward in the right direction.

Also, as I neither smoke nor drink, I have few regular 'personal' expenses. I also work a lot at my 'day job', (psychologist, psychotherapist), so I can afford to invest the resources needed.

These types of reflections happen to all of us, and we need to be prepared to cross these dark nights of the soul'.

I remember quite a few discussions with my wife during the last years of her studies of medicine, when she was questioning her choices and motivation to finish them.

She was also wondering whether it was worthwhile to complete her training.

It is not questioning your choices that is a problem, quite the opposite, it is a healthy thing to do.

It is already being prepared, yourself and or your closest friends, to have convincing arguments of why it is reasonable to continue.

However, you might not have enough convincing arguments to undertake a long and difficult path.

You might not feel that you have either the opportunity, motivation, capacity or interest to invest to aim for anything other than an alimentary job, one that 'just' succeeds to feed, clothe and house you.

And that can also be totally okay!

2.3 Why do I work?

Fame & Fortune Or Fun, Family & Friends?

What do I want and need from working?

Not enough of us ask the question of 'why do we work?', and 'what do we want to get out of working?'

These questions are fundamental for finding a work that satisfies our basic; wants, needs and desires.

Do you want / need to be; the most rich, powerful, person in your profession, so you can force the world to bend to your will?

Do you want to prove to yourself, and / or others, that you can succeed in something, because you can then look at them / yourself in the mirror, and say, 'see, no matter what you thought, I've made it'?

Or, are you more of the; 'I work because I need to keep a roof over my / my family's head, food in one's stomach, and clothes on one's back'?

As with everything in life, nothing is that black and white, and most of us live somewhere across several continua. (Yes, that is the plural of continuum, I looked it up).

'Be the best. Mediocracy is for losers.'

This is a reality drummed into many of us, from a very early age.

Yes, many of us live in very competitive worlds, and if we don't battle from the first grade of school, we might well be doomed to that awful world of mediocrity.

But just how much is it worth to invest?

In researching this topic, I found a wonderful answer to this question:

'What is the point of living an unexceptional life?', on the Quora forum by ***Eivind Kjørstad***
[3](Updated Jan 16, 2016)

"I live an entirely unexceptional life. Listen.

I'm a pretty average-looking 39-year-old guy. I've got a decent education, but nothing out of the ordinary.

I've got a decent job that I enjoy doing, but it's nothing earth-shaking. I'm married to a woman who means the world to me, but who has not thus far won either the Nobel Prize or Miss Universe, nor is she, I reckon, likely to ever do so.

I've got 3 kids. They're healthy and happy children who do fairly well in school and have several hobbies they love. They mean the world to me, too, but thus far none of them have won the Nobel Prize either, nor do I have any particular reason to believe that they will.

---

[3] https://www.quora.com/What-is-the-point-of-living-an-unexceptional-life/answer/Eivind-Kj%C3%B8rstad retrieved 25.06.2017

I've got perhaps a dozen friends that I love, and a larger count of acquaintances of varying closeness. I live in a perfectly ordinary Norwegian house, and drive a 12-year-old Toyota that hasn't been washed this month.

None of this is exceptional to anyone except for me.

This is my life and I happen to enjoy it very much. Actually, that is an understatement; if you'd told me a couple of decades ago that I'd be as happy as I am, I'd have refused to believe you.

From MY perspective, I've got everything anyone could possible want. Health. Hobbies. Friends. And Love.

I'm not exceptional in any of these things; but why would I need to be?

The rewards I desire don't seem unreachable to me. On the contrary, I feel like being alive right now, just like this, it is reward enough. What more could I need?

I'm going to turn off the computer now, then I'm going to find a bottle of wine for when my wife returns later; and spend the 45 minutes until then playing the guitar.

 I do this because it's fun, because it's challenging, because I love learning and I love music, and because I can.

That's my life. It's not an exceptional one.

But my biggest regret is that I'm unlikely to get much more than 50 additional years of it. I intend to do my very best to enjoy every single day of it though."

1m Views · 21,679 Upvotes

Please don't get me wrong; striving for success, emulating excellence and pursuing perfection are still wonderful and noble aspirations.

If nobody would choose to take on these roles, then there would be no new inventions, industries or systems.

We need, without question; the captains of industry, the leaders of countries, the explorers of science, knowledge and new paradigms.

However, it just isn't for everyone.

2.4 Predators and prey

In the animal kingdom, there are two basics types of creatures; predators and prey.

It is simple enough to divide the two; predators have their eyes in the front of their heads and are carnivorous, while prey have their eyes on the sides of their heads and are herbivores.

Predators have excellent binocular vision so that they can easily target their food.

Prey have poor binocular vision, but excellent peripheric vision so that they can see predators from any direction from which they might attack.

We humans also divide, (more or less), into predators or prey.

Predators, (alphas, leaders, perfectionists, high performers), can be; single minded, highly focused, unemphatic, incredibly hard working and driven people.

They have many characteristics that western society would consider as 'male'.

Prey, (carers, supporters, helpers, enablers), are likely to be; team players, multitaskers, sensitive and empathic. What one would generally call 'female' traits.

Of course, most of us have traits of both types, and we rarely meet people that are totally extreme in one or the other.

However, almost all politicians, top athletes and captains of industry are predators.

And many nurses, teachers, nuns and monks, would easily fit into the group of prey.

There is no right or wrong in being predator or prey.

Clearly, being on the extreme of any type of group brings very particular challenges; on one hand, not to abuse those weaker than yourself, on the other, not to allow yourself to be totally abused by the strong and powerful.

What is worth reflecting on, is where on the continua, am I between predator and prey?

And what does that tell me about the type of work and the investment in that work, which is appropriate to me?

Fame or Riches, (no, they are not necessarily linked), can be worth striving for. However, the cost can be enormous.

In general, if you aim for either of these goddesses, they will demand that you marry them.

For they will expect, no they will demand, an investment and a fidelity of the highest order.

And these bitches, for that is what they are, even if you succeed to capture them, will offer you pride and success, but not necessarily happiness.

However, there are those of us, that can aim for nothing lower, and all power to you. We need our heroes, even if most of you won't make it, and will be found, laying, dying in the trenches.

Then there are the idealists and artists, these are those for whom their work is their expression of themselves.

Be they writers, teachers, dancers, musicians, film makers, doctors, nurses, researchers, teachers, painters, singers, inventors, and every person, for whom their work is their passion.

These are amongst the happiest and the saddest of humanity. To be able to live their obsession, is all that they want and need.

However, even if they seem to succeed to put into place a professional life that responds to these desires, it can still often turn sour.

My father, who, at the time, was in his first years of being a professional musician, succeeded to get a 3 months contract to play in a 'holiday camp'.

He was given a house and a decent wage for himself and the rest of his band. Unfortunately, after only one week, he was ready to quit.

The music that they were instructed to play, was much too boring for them.

At the end, he was 'forced' to drive a mini car, round and round the inside of the ball room, during a board meeting, to get himself fired!!!!! (True story)

Many nurses that I know complain that they cannot correctly look after their patients, the administration won't allow them the time.

However, those that can find a professional identity that fits with their inner identity, are (front their point of view), the most blessed of this earth.

My 'day job', is that of a psychologist, psychotherapist. It totally fits with a part of my 'prey' personality, and my days, although often long and tiring, are most satisfying.

Of course, these are far from the majority of the world's population. The vast majority of us, have to content ourselves with being satisfied to feed and clothe ourselves and our families.

And, as long as this is okay, then there is no shame in this. In fact, in general, those that aim for and succeed this are the most content of folks.

This is where we return to that 'dangerous' position of accepting and embracing mediocrity.

So, want is better, best?

The answer, that I hope you've already well captured, is, 'what-ever works best for you.'

Finding your own path, independent of the persuasive pressures of family and friends, is not always easy to do.

But it is a most important reflection to make before you can successfully continue.

Once you have advanced on that reflection, now would be a good time to put that into practice, and go and get a training or a job.

3 Step 2 – Getting a job

3.1 Opening up to getting a job

Yes, you say that you want a job, but are you open to getting one?

It seems like a daft question, if one doesn't have a job, or is unhappy with the one that they have, surely, they will be open to getting a (new) one.

Strangely enough, this is often not the case.

To really be in the right state you need to open; your mouth, your ears, your eyes and your mind.

Open mouth; communicate to everyone that you might meet that you are looking to find a job. (Obviously, if you are still employed you might have to be a little discrete about this).

Open your ears; listen to what people are saying, ask them questions, find out more information.

Open your eyes; look to see what is possibly available.

Open your mind; be ready to try something that you hadn't thought of before or that you are not totally sure that you can do.

3.2 Theo, the shipping clerk.

Theo had worked for the same company, in the same job, for most of his life.

"I'm bored," he would complain to me, "I'm thinking of handing in my notice and quitting the place."

"It's a big company, aren't there any other positions that you could try for?" I queried.

"No, there are sometimes jobs posted on the internal notice boards, but as I'm not trained in anything other than my job, it's not even worth thinking about."

"Listen," I suggested, "as you are anyway thinking of handing in your notice, what would you have to lose if you went and discussed this with your supervisor?"

Theo stopped and thought for a second before replying.

"Yeh, why not? You're right, I've really nothing to lose, I'm already ready to leave, and if they sack me, I won't get penalised by the unemployment for quitting the job."

The next time I saw him, I asked if he had, had the chance to talk to his boss.

He stood shaking his head.

"So, you didn't get to speak to him, then?"

"Yeh, I did speak to him, and he seems happy that I did."

Not understanding why he had shaken his head, I pressed on.

"So, what was wrong?"

"He said that he had been waiting for me to ask, and that he had already suggested several times that I think to try something else."

"But you never told me this," I remarked.

"I thought that he has unsatisfied with my work, and was threatening to sack me."

"But he wasn't."

"No, he said that they, whoever they might be, had been thinking for a while that I was too competent for the job that I do."

"And?"

"That I could do something more interesting."

"So, why did you shake your head just now?"

"Well he went off to talk to his supervisor, who is responsible for mine and a few other departments."

"And?"

"And he called me into his office a few days later and offered me another job."

"But?"

"But it's something with much more responsibility, and I've never done anything like it before. So, I'm sure that I could never do it."

"But your boss's boss thinks that you can."

"Well, he's likely to be wrong."

"After all the years that you've worked there, maybe he has reason to think that you could do this new job."

"Do you really think so?"

"Yes, yes I do."

"Okay then."

I don't see Theo for some weeks.

"So what happened about the job?"

"As they say in 'Aussi' land, 'no worries'".

"So, it worked out then?"

"The guy that was doing the job was retiring. So, they gave me loads of time to sit with him while he showed me all the details of the job.

And, any time that I might have any questions, he says that I can call him up, and he has even promised to come back, from time to time, if I might need him to explain something."

"And your bosses are okay with that?"

" 'Course they are, it seems that they even suggested it."

This is taken from a true story.

Theo, (of course not his real name), although, more and more unhappy with his job, hadn't dared to open up to getting a new job.

He had refused to talk to anyone about his frustration with his current post.

Hence, there was no chance of any feedback.

He saw, but didn't really see, the job openings that were on offer.

Because, he couldn't open his mind to the idea that he might be capable to do something different.

3.3 Allied Records

My first university studies were in Management and Administrative Sciences, for which we were obliged to find a one-year work experience, (internship), in industry.

The university had linked with many different companies, and throughout our second year there were lists of job opportunities pinned on a notice board of job offers.

Underneath each job offer was a place for students, if interested to enter their names. At some point, a representative of that company would come to Aston, and hold interviews for that job.

Every day there would be a type of rugby scrum in front of the notice board, to see what new jobs where being offered and to sign up for an interview.

As I couldn't find any jobs that really interested me, I finally wrote my name down for working for a supermarket chain, but almost immediately regretted it.

After I found out, (to my great relief), that I hadn't been selected for an interview, I realised that this wasn't going to work for me, and stopped bothering to even go to check out the new job offers.

Unfortunately, finding a job was a necessary requirement for finishing my degree, but I was optimistic that I would find something.

After the end of the academic year I returned home, and discussed the situation with my parents.

My father had a friend that owned a large accountancy firm, and he was sure that he could find me a position there.

As I had already had the opportunity to work there for a one-week experience, I was clear that, that would be a torture that would be impossible to endure for another week, never mind a whole year.

'I'll sort it out,' I cheerfully assured them.

I then phoned up the London Times, (we were living in Blackpool, in the North West of the UK at that time), and placed an advert looking for a job.

As the Times was very expensive, and as I had hardly any savings, I could only afford for the ad to appear once.

I placed the ad and went off working away from home with my father.

Some nights later, I phoned my mother to ask if there was any response from the advert and she informed me that I had a job.

How could I have a job when I've not even spoken to the guy?

It turns out that the man, Marcel Rod, the owner of Allied Records, was an old business acquaintance of my father's. And although he hadn't realised it at the time, my mother recognised his voice, and he offered me the job based on his appreciation of my parents.

However, things didn't work out as planned and after five months on the job, I was fired.

As I was happy living in London, and I didn't wish to return to Lancashire, I found a temporary job working in the warehouse of Hamley's toy shop, up until the Christmas holidays.

When the university found out that I had lost my management trainee job, they immediately phoned my parents and threatened that I would be thrown off from my course, if I didn't find a new trainee post in the next few weeks.

My parents then drove down to London, to collect me and bring me back up north.

(Un)fortunately I was out at work and didn't come home all day, so reluctantly, they had to give up and return back home.

When I found out that they had been looking for me, I called them up and succeeded to negotiate with them, that if I hadn't secured a new traineeship by the end of the year, then I would return home and go and work for the accountant, (ugh!).

The next day I called up the human resources department and asked for an interview.

Several days later I was informed by the supervisor of the warehouse that I was to go with the next van into town, and go up to HR office.

So, there I was, a temporary, warehouse helper, dressed in dirty jeans and shirt, going to the HR department, to convince them to give me a management trainee position.

They listened patiently to my story and to my proposition to transfer to a traineeship in their toyshop.

They even seemed sympathetic, but then they reflected that it was difficult and even costly for them to employ someone that had been 'introduced' through a temporary agency.

"We'll think about it and let you know. Thank you for your time."

And that was that. The last weeks before Christmas came and went, but with no further news from the HR people.

It was Christmas eve, everyone was saying their Happy Christmas's and their goodbye's. I had left the warehouse and was on the road, back, unfortunately to Lancashire and an accountant's office.

When I was called back by the warehouse supervisor.

"Oh, Gary, do you know where you are supposed to go?"

"Go? Go where?"

"You are to report to the HR department on the 2nd of January at 9.00am, Happy Christmas!"

I stopped for a second and looked at him blankly.

He then repeated the message, not being sure if I was deaf or stupid.

"Thank you, I finally responded, "and have a great Christmas, yourself."

I went, in one magic moment, from being the black sheep of the Industrial Placements at university, who didn't bother to sign up for any jobs.

And to be the first and only student to get sacked from his placement.

To being the student star, who managed to get, not one, but two placements, by his own means, and opened up Hamley's toyshop of Regent's street, as new placement employer.

3.4 Reflexions on being open.

These are both true stories, and that was exactly what happened during my industrial placement year.

In my case, I dared to reject the placements that had been offered because none of them appealed to me.

I had several interviews with the placement officer, who tried to convince me to apply for one job or another, but nothing interested me.

So, I just didn't bother.

In both cases the person accepted to open their 'mouths'; Theo, to talk to his boss, myself, once by advertising in the Times, once through demanding an interview with the HR department.

I had seen how busy the sales assistants were working and was convinced, with many years of experience in direct selling, that I could be of service.

We then both listened to what was offered.

Then we opened our minds, (I had never thought of working as a trainee assistant manager in a record pressing factory), and accepted the challenge of the job offered.

When asking for the job at Hamley's, I very clearly stated that I was willing to do anything that they might ask of me, as long as it satisfied the requirements of my university traineeship.

So, if you want a job – open up.

3.5 Shrinking or stretching?

When looking for a job, we often have an industry or a type of business in which we would like to work, but cannot always find a job that exactly meets our academic training and work experience.

Some people think that to take a job, any job in that workplace, even if we are overqualified for it, is a good idea as it gets us into that organisation.

Sorry, but the days of working one's way up the corporate ladder seem to be over.

Not only are the chances of being noticed by your bosses and handed more and more interesting tasks nigh on impossible.

Not only that, but working under someone that has less qualification, experience or aptitude than you have, is a pure recipe for disaster.

While working at Hamley's, the floor manager was relieved of her duties as she was about to have a baby, and the assistant manager had temporary responsibility for the sales floor, where I was working.

Unfortunately, I had, had much more sales experience than her and I often didn't agree with the tasks that she gave me.

After several weeks of asking me to do things, where I would; confirm several times whether she was sure that she wanted me to do the thing.

Then I would dutifully start the designated task, but quite soon, I would find many, many more important things to do, until it became obvious that I would never complete it.

Hence, she would either have to ask someone else, or finish it herself.

It took a few weeks to 'train' her not to try to force me to do stuff that I didn't agree to do.

Fortunately, she was not an aggressive type, and didn't give me a hard time over it. (And I had become quite friendly with the 'buyer' for the floor, who was sort of her boss's boss).

This is not a strategy that I would suggest to follow, as it could finish rather badly with any other type of superior than her.

In my many holiday and temporary jobs, I have regularly come up against this type of problem.

So, if shrinking down, to get a job, is not a good idea, how about stretching up?

Many people, like Theo, are too intimidated to apply for jobs because they fear that they are not qualified or experienced enough to assume them.

Strangely enough, whether you are capable or not to do a job, is neither your problem, nor your responsibility.

Your only real responsibility, when applying for a job, is to be honest.

Of course, writing a CV must be creative affair, highlighting everything that you can do or have done, that might be of interest to the recruiter, and downplaying anything that might seem negative.

However, when it comes to your specific training and skills, never, ever lie!

Yes, be positive, be upbeat, be as convincing as you possibly can be about who you are and what you can do, but never say that you can do something that you know that you cannot do.

The more that you are honest about the level of your training, skills and experience, the more the responsibility of employing you falls on the shoulders of interviewer.

If they believe that you can do the job, then trust their knowledge and experience, and allow yourself to stretch up and grow into it.

When I first arrived in Switzerland, I couldn't find any work. This was not so surprising as I neither spoke the language nor had a work permit.

And so, I started to get depressed.

This was at the same time that my wife was undertaking her trainee year as part of her medical studies.

She came across a list of institutions that offered short internships for future psychologists.

And as I was planning to begin studies in psychology, she thought that I might be able to get a temporary post in one of these places.

So, she got to work writing job applications in my name.

Quite quickly I got a job interview. It was for a three-month job working in a children's home.

The interview was held in English, and the guy seemed quite taken with me, but I was very nervous to accept the offer.

"But I can hardly speak any French," I admitted.

"Do you speak, 'children'?"

"Yes, I think that I can communicate with kids."

"Then it will be fine."

-   And it was.

I always carried my pocket bilingual dictionary with me, and the kids had great fun teaching me bits of French.

So, as long as you are honest about your experience and abilities, do not hesitate to apply for jobs that you are not totally sure that you can do. Let your future employer decide if they believe that you are a good fit and if they are willing to help you to grow into the position.

3.6 How much are you worth?

When seeking a job, especially when it is your first job, or if you've been out of work for some time, it can seem to be a reasonable idea to accept poor pay and or poor work conditions, (expected but unpaid overtime, less than standard holidays, etc.), in your desire to get employed.

Many unscrupulous employers will suggest that they are doing you a favour to employ you, and you should be appreciative that you are even considering you.

It must be admitted that in certain parts of the world, and depending on your real 'worth', (qualifications, training, experience), you might truly be lucky to get any job, because there really are many, equally qualified people that would be happy to have this place, and that you have few arguments to demand better treatment.

In these cases, it is important to be either ready to accept that unpleasant reality, or find some means to change it.

Change it could mean getting a more unique qualification or skill, or thinking to create your own enterprise, or leaving the area altogether.

- Remember, we are dealing with the real world here, not just some theoretical fantasyland.

Fortunately, I believe, that most people reading this book, are not in that position, and do have the means to negotiate a more equitable employment agreement.

However, an employer is in the business of earning profits, and many would not hesitate to exploit someone particularly eager to find a job.

"I'm doing you a favour employing you. If I hadn't created this business, there would be no job for you, so accept what I am offering."

3.7 Toad Transport

Thomas Toad owned a transport company. He had a big, old wooden cart with the words 'Thomas Toad Transport', bravely painted on it. The cart was drawn by four horses, organised in two rows of two.

Thomas had a very, very big family and had to work hard to feed them all, but as he was a responsible husband, and really enjoyed his work, that wasn't too much of a problem.

The problem was the horses, it seemed that they didn't enjoy the work quite as much as he did, and as they had no families to feed, they were, understandably rather less motivated.

Also, their lives were not that paradisiac. They were either working or they were imprisoned in their narrow boxes, eating, sleeping or just waiting to go to work.

They were given enough hay to stay on form, and from time to time, if Toad was feeling in a good mood, a few handful of oats.

Even though they were not happy with their lives, they were much too afraid to complain.

They had all seen, or at least had heard speak of, a horse that had started to complain about their living conditions, that had been driven away in the butcher's van!

And they all knew of the butcher's shiny white van, with, 'Billy Bulldog Butcher – Cow, Sheep and Horse' threateningly, splashed across in blood, red letters.

They knew of it, as it was the first thing that they saw when herded of the cattle boat, arriving in this cold, sad country.

The second waggon, was that of Mr. Toad, who was quick to offer to save them from slaughter, if they would choose to come and work for him.

Too afraid to wait and take the chance that no other employer would show up, the strong, healthy beasts would, more than willingly indenture themselves to lifelong, work agreement for their generous saviour.

However, the saving of their lives was quickly replaced by a life of servitude, with only the vague promise of a peaceful retirement if they would work as he wished them to.

Some of the horses were even of the opinion that the 'peaceful retirement' would take place in the local glue factory, they had so little trust in their puffed up, green employer.

Until one day in early spring …

Mr. Toad was to pick up some cargo from a village quite some ways away and so they set out very early in the morning.

He had spent some time explaining the route to Horace, the lead horse, as he planned to go back to sleep in the back of the cart, as they were leaving so early in the morning.

This was something that happened from time to time, and Horace would whinny just before they would get into town, so that Toad could take up the reigns before anyone would see them.

The day proved to be warm and sunny, and although, from time to time, Toad half woke from his sleep, as Horace had not yet called, he just turned over and continued his slumbers, pleasantly rocked by the gentle swaying of the old waggon.

Finally, as with all of us, Toad needed to pee.

The call of nature, being as it is, forced him to wake up and take stock of his surroundings.

"Where are we?" He called out to Horace. He felt a little concerned, as this being a road that he didn't know well, seemed to be different than he remembered it to be.

"On the road," cheerfully called back the lead horse.

"Are you sure that it's the right road?"

"This is exactly where we should be heading."

"But it doesn't look familiar to me. Stop a moment and we'll look at the map."

"Sorry boss, no can do."

"What do you mean, 'no can do'? No horse had ever spoken to him like that.

"No can do. Just sit back down and see where that gets you."

"No, I will not." He started to get irritated, his neck was beginning to puff up. "You will do exactly as I say. Stop the cart!"

"Sorry, no can do," only this time it was the mare, Hermine, that repeated the denial.

"We'll see about that;" Toad jumped up and grabbed the reins, pulling them back with all the force and violence that he could muster.

Only they met with no resistance. Instead of biting the hard, metal bits against the horse's tender mouths, the worn, leather straps, flew back towards the shocked amphibian.

The brisk movement whipped the cords backwards, violently slashing across the lumpy, head and face.

At some moment in the morning, the horses had managed to release the clasps that attached the reins to the bridles.

"Stop, stop. I command you." His neck was now totally ballooned out.

The worse of responses, the horses just whinnied to each other and ignored him.

Toad was forced to stagger to the back of the cart, nature would wait no longer, and humiliated, he peed, standing up, where anyone could see.

After that, he had no choice but to just sit and wait to see what would happen. They were travelling miles and miles away from anywhere that he had ever been in his long life.

What did they want? What could they possibly hope to benefit from taking everyone so very far from anywhere they knew?

Finally, as the sun was setting, the horses finally tired to a standstill.

"Now what, you stupid beasts? It's nearly night, and we are lost in the middle of nowhere. What have your little, stupid minds thought would happen now? There's nothing to eat and nowhere to sleep."

"Not, maybe for you."

The horses slipped out of the wooden traces, which dropped heavily onto the dusty road. They then ambled over to wild meadow and started to graze.

"You see, we have all that we could possibly want and need right here. Grass to eat, rivers from which to drink, trees to shelter us from the rain, and we sleep where we choose."

"But what about me? What am I supposed to eat? How am I supposed to get home? What am I going to do?" Toad started to feel weak, lost and, for the first time in his proud life, scared.

"What do you want from us?" Horace smiled, as he asked the question.

Toad stopped to reflect on his answer. Even when he knew what he had to say, it took him quite a while before he could force himself to allow the miserable horse to hear it.

"I need you," mumbled.

"Sorry, didn't quite catch that."

"I .. need .. you!" The distraught toad screamed in anger and despair.

"Just you remember that when you are paying the ship owner for transporting your new team of horses.

"Just remember that when you are working them seven days a week.

"Just remember that when you keep them locked up in their minimum, legal sized boxes, all the rest of the time.

"Just remember that, and maybe this won't happen again."

"Yes, I suppose I must," and so the old and maybe a little wiser toad, got down off of the waggon and started walking, back along the long, long road back to his home.

3.8 Getting in

So how do you convince a perspective employer to take you on without opening yourself to being exploited?

In the retail trade, it is not uncommon to be given free samples or special offers to attract new customers.

As a prospective new, untested employee, it would not be unreasonable to offer to work for a limited time free or if that is not possible, for a minimum salary.

If you agree that you are lacking in qualifications or specific experience, you could offer to work for a reduced salary until you have gained those qualifications and experience.

What is essential in such a situation is for the time for which you are unpaid, or paid less than you feel you are / will be worth, is very clearly defined.

The employment contract is one of the most important contracts in our lives, and we need to be sure that it is acceptable before we sign it.

As it is the employer that creates it, and we are presented with it to sign, it seems difficult, if not impossible to change things, especially as we are most keen to get the job.

Don't!

Do not sign the contract in that moment of pressure, of duress.

Insist on taking it home, promise to return with it signed in the next few days, but give yourself the time and space to look at it, (with others), in the quiet and comfort of your own home.

One of the things that I remember from a course in contract law, that I took, over 40 years ago, was the simple idea, that if there is something in a contract that doesn't suit, then change it.

If something doesn't work for you, then cross it out and write in what you think is reasonable for you. The fact that it is a pretty, printed document, in no way means that you cannot change it.

Then, when you are satisfied with it, then you can fulfil your promise to return with the document duly signed.

There is likely to be a reaction from your perspective employer.

If he insists on keeping in clauses that you really are not happy with, then, honestly, you had better, seriously question yourself; 'is worth to enter into a work relationship that already shows signs of dysfunctioning?'

However, sometimes the cost-benefit of being in a job where we are clearly being exploited can still be positive.

Finishing studying psychology in Switzerland is already quite a challenge, but finding an internship, first job, is awfully difficult.

I had the incredible good fortune to have already found an unpaid trainee position during my final year of studies.

And, as I needed a place to work for my research to complete my Master's, he accepted to keep me on.

The work conditions were not optimal; I shared a cupboard sized workspace with another young psychologist, my boss was often irritable and unpleasant with me, and worst of the worst, even though he billed the insurance companies for my work, he didn't pay me anything!!!

To be strictly honest, after four months of work and empty promises and a loud, stand up row between us, (yes, I shouted at him), he finally agreed to pay me a percentage for each consultation that I undertook.

Abusive, yes, there can be no questions there.

But, ask me now, looking back, if I would make the same choice again, to go and work there, in exactly the same conditions, for him, my response would be – yes, yes, and yes!

Although mean with money and with patience, he was incredibly generous with sharing his knowledge and expertise.

He was one of the original practitioners of hypnosis in our part of the world, and wonderful with it.

He was also the most known and respected systemic – family therapists in the 'state'.

The knowledge, experience and confidence in myself as a therapist all came from the opening that he offered me.

Also, the opportunity to run groups, both on my own, and later with my wife, (who came to work with him as well), and for the support to research and present my Master's thesis, (for which I got a 1st), – thank you Gerard.

So, you also need to weigh-up all the costs and benefits of working for a person / enterprise / institution.

It might be more worthwhile than you might initially think.

3.9 Written and Unwritten Conditions

A short reflection on what I term, 'unwritten work conditions'.

In many industries; medicine, advertising, many areas of upper management, and research, as well as certain countries; the U.S. and Japan, for instance, there are 'norms', that go beyond the wording in any contract.

In these types of work environments, it is totally expected that you work well over and above the hours specified in your contract.

So, what to do in these circumstances?

First and foremost, be clear what the real expectations of your work supervisors expect.

Hence, before entering, in one of your employment interviews, ask, in writing, (always), for a clear limitation of your work contract.

If your future employer is honest enough to share with you that your contract is as offered to you, but, in reality, it is poorly looked on to limit your working hours / weeks to that.

To; leave before 9pm, or not work one weekend out of two, or, that although you have the right to five weeks holiday a year, if you take more than three, your job will surely be in jeopardy.

In this case, you have three options; either take the job, knowing and accepting the conditions of the unwritten contract, don't take the job, just walk away, or renegotiate those conditions.

I have an American friend, (hi Andy), that took one of those jobs in which he officially had five weeks holiday per year, but the industry norm was only two or exceptionally three.

As his wife is French, and it was their habit to spend four weeks per year with her family in France, and still take a week off for Christmas, to spend it with his family, he renegotiated his unwritten contract.

It was known and accepted by all levels of management that he would be taking his legal, written contractual vacation allowance.

And so, that is what happened.

I also had, (surprise, surprise), a work experience that comes under the same heading, but as I will be mentioning it later on, (Chapter 4.6, The Busy Beaver), it is not worth retelling it twice.

Just remember, every contract, written, oral or tacit, should be explicitly understand and accepted, or rejected, or changed, if possible, before you agree to it.

Section 2 – Your Co-workers, Bosses and Subordinates

General introduction to this section.

How to deal with those that you are forced to function with at work, is not always easy or obvious.

In this second section, I have tried to suggest various attitudes and approaches as to how best to work with these colleagues.

If sometimes it seems that I leave the path of spiritual purity, for this I cannot apologise. My aim is to help people find a means to cope with real world situations.

Situations that are often unjust and unfair.

Life is often twisted to our disadvantage, if you cannot, do not, or choose not to twist it a little to bring it back into some sort of balance, then you will either be a victim or a saint.

For those of us who cannot or choose not to be one or the other of the above, this section is for you.

4. Your Co-workers

4.1 Colleagues – First Encounters

Our colleagues are likely to be the people we spend the most time with at work.

In truth, they might be the people that we spend the most time with in our daily lives.

So, it is very important to succeed, as much as possible to get on with them.

When entering any new group there are a series of steps to follow to assure, as much as possible that it passes well.

The three steps are; observation, imitation, integration.

Observation: You arrive on day one; no matter what your job is, or what level you have in the hierarchy of the organisation, do not try and impose your vision of the universe on the people already there.

Every group already has its systems in place; how things are done, who does what, the roles that each person assumes.

Come in, do your assigned tasks and observe how the system that you have entered functions.

Even if you are coming in at a high level, these three steps still apply to you. – However, for managers, there is a 4th step, 'Re-creation', but that we will reflect on further on.

If you come 'with your big boots', there is a high probability that you will be seen and felt as a threat to the group's functioning, and will be attacked as a way to protect the integrity of the group.

During this phase, by keeping a low profile, but a high level of vigilance, you will able to perceive how each person operates.

Who are the friendly ones, the (un)official leaders, the distant ones, the opinionated ones, the greedy, the lazy, the manipulators, but most of all, the protected.

The protected are of course the most dangerous. These are the colleagues, who, for some reason or other, social or professional links, have someone higher up in the hierarchy that they know will protect them if they might have any problems.

These are the people to whom the usual rules of the institution do not always apply, and that gives them a dangerous power.

Whether they ever choose to use or abuse this power, of course, depends entirely on the person.

I have met and worked with many people that were very close to the owners, who never, ever used that contact to their advantage nor to my disadvantage.

Imitation: No, this doesn't mean pretending to be one of your colleagues. What it does mean is to not express any views or behaviours that are not clearly acceptable to the others.

If they are saying of doing something that you are not agreeing with, keep it to yourself, for now.

Integration: This is the moment when you feel that you are accepted into the group for who you are.

Now is the time to start to express your opinions, and even try to persuade other members to follow your ideas and ideals.

To give a real example of this process.

Many, many years ago, I had a temporary job filling envelopes with a large number of other 'temps'.

This was moment of the first privatization of a public utilities company in the UK, I think that it was selling shares in British Gas, which would make it 1986.

Observation:
I was assigned to sit at one of a number of large round tables, where we passed our days in this highly intellectual task.

And so, I joined a table of people, of which a 'group of colleagues' had already been formed.

It took a day or so to feel comfortable enough to join in the conversations, and to see what they were doing.

What some of them were doing was to write 'humorous' messages on the forms that we were stuffing the envelopes with.

What was even more problematic was that I found out that they had a way to steal from the vending machine in the refractory.

Imitation:
Even though I was not comfortable with either the remarks added to the forms, but mainly to the fact that they were stealing from the machine, to begin with, although I certainly didn't participate in it, I didn't say or do anything either.

Integration:
After a few more days, I felt that I had found my place in the group, and that it was now time that I expressed my position on the way that the group was behaving.

I chose to ignore the messages, as most of the group found it an amusing distraction in what was a mind destroying, boring job. And as I didn't think that it was likely to do much harm, I chose not to risk being ostracized over that.

However, going into the refractory with those members of the group who were stealing from the machine, I warned them that, as we were all part of the same crew, if the people responsible found out that our team were stealing, I and other innocent colleagues would all be suspected.

Stealing was already not acceptable to me, but the risk that I and others might be suspected of theft was out of the question.

Hence, I informed them, if I saw or heard that they had stolen one more chocolate bar, I would denounce them myself.

Of course, the stealing stopped, and that was that.

4.2 The sad, slow snail

We have all met in life slow and lazy people. In our social lives, we might find them; irritating, frustrating, maybe even faintly amusing, but these characteristics in a work colleague, are no laughing matter.

As with most troublesome members of your team, it is always a good idea to distance yourself, as far as possible from the negative effects of their none productivity.

However, these people are often also the most awful moaners. Their lives are often strewn with difficulties and problems.

They would really like to be more productive, but due to; poor health, personal problems or some other type of catastrophe, they are just not able to, at this moment in time.

They are the kings and queens of the inevitable guilt trip.

The first thing to keep in mind is, if possible, never do any work in their place.

This is the most likely reaction if you find yourself blocked because your work depends on theirs.

Especially if you are a normal, caring person.

Don't do it!

These people thrive on getting others to do their work for them.

And will likely end up with you doing most of their work as well as your own.

Anyway, if the quantity of work that you are expected to produce is appropriate for your working schedule, then it should be impossible for you to do both their job and yours.

If you have to support them to do work which then feeds yours, it is logical that the work that will not get finished will be the stuff that you are expected to produce.

In that case, it will be you that looks bad, and not them.

So, what to do?

Ask your boss if he wishes for you to help them, repeating their excuses for not succeeding to do their work.

Write, (always, always, always leave a written trace, where possible, for any exchange that you have at work), in the most sympathetic, caring, and helpful tone that you can.

Explaining how it cannot be their fault that they are so unproductive, but just the same, it is blocking you from completing your own tasks.

And so, if your boss would wish for you to officially take over some of their tasks, then you would be most ready to do so.

However, that would mean that your own work might not be finished as planned.

Or, if he would prefer, you could focus on some other tasks, while you are waiting for your colleagues to finish theirs, but, by the same rule, your planning would still need to be officially updated.

No matter what your manager decides, all that is really important, is that you have covered your own back, and cannot, reasonably be criticised for being late with your own work.

This would be equally true, even if your manager doesn't think to respond.

To have already signalled the problem means that it is now your manager's responsibility if you fail to meet your work quota.

4.3 The bitch

The bitch is an interesting creature, (note, men can also be bitches, we just call them be other names).

She is often; rude, unpleasant, irritable and given a wide berth by most people, when they get the chance.

She might also be; intelligent, hardworking, perfectionist and (unfortunately), much appreciated by her boss.

Often, she might also display a sharp and malicious sense of humour.

She might be; young, beautiful, sexy, stuck-up and much appreciated by members of the opposite sex, but she might be, just as easily, old, fat, ugly and, (not so surprisingly), painfully single.

Newsflash – she is not your enemy. (Unless you are lazy and / or incompetent).

Don't let her nastiness intimidate you.

Do your work well and conscientiously and you can expect her to be your ally.

Yes, she will expect you to treat her with a certain politeness and respect, but do it as an equal.

She will not respect you if you do not stand up to her.

However, she can be both loyal and protective.

As she is neither dishonest nor cowardly, if she feels that there is an injustice against someone that she holds in esteem, she will defend them.

4.4 Miss Vera Pitkin-Hammond

Miss Vera Pitkin-Hammond was, I believe, the head of bookkeeping for Hamley's Toyshop. She was also the bane of the lives of many people that worked there.

Towards the end of my traineeship, (internship), at Hamley's I was on the administrative floor, in the role of a 'buyer's assistant'.

For some reason or other, all the other assistants were young women.

We had the job to keep the accounts of all the toys that the buyer had ordered and to communicate the numbers to the accounts department.

Several times in the few weeks that I was on that floor, I found an assistant in floods of tears.

She had, had a phone call from VP-H, and had been violently insulted for messing up the weekly report.

I was meant to work with my buyer for some weeks, but she got a call from the HR that the accounts department was short-handed and could I cut short my work with her and for me to report to VP-H that very afternoon.

The other assistants all but gave me the 'last rites'.

I arrived just after lunch to find the dragon lady entering with a ….. birthday cake!

It was her assistant's birthday and so she had thought to buy both a card and a cake.

That didn't change the fact that, on average, once a week, her assistant was in tears because she had been rudely criticised for some error or other that she had committed.

Miss Vera Pitkin-Hammond, (and woe betide you if you addressed her simply as Miss Hammond!!), was about 50 years old, legs like tree trunks, heavily bandaged against Lord knows what, smoked like a chimney, and had a tongue that was sharp enough to cut through the thickest of thick skins.

She never ceased to attack me, but, although always polite, I never buckled, and she loved that.

For the last anecdote.

It was a Friday afternoon, I had finished the job assigned to me, and so I thought that I might as well call it a day.

"Have a nice weekend," I called out on passing her work station.

"Mr. Gedall, are you aware of what time it is?"

Checking my watch, "it's five forty."

"And what time do we finish work?"

"At five fifty," at this point, most people would have already removed their coats and be returning to their desks. "Would you like me to do something else before I go?"

"No, I was simply checking that you were aware of the time. Have a nice weekend."

Smiling to herself, she returned punching in numbers on her old, mechanical adding machine.

And that was Miss Vera Pitkin-Hammond, the Dragon-lady of Hamley's accounting department.

4.5 The lost cause

Every so often, in some area of our lives, we come across, a 'lost cause'.

Someone who's life; financial, relationship and, or, health, (their own or someone close), is a constant, invading, challenge.

They are often particularly nice, kind, friendly and supportive of all those around them, but for themselves, never seem to find, that one specific thing, person, solution that will help them to escape their own problems.

And so, they turn to you to help. 'I'm sure that you could be the one that will succeed to rescue me from the badness of my life.'

It is so gratifying and ego-boosting to image that humble me, might, when all-else have failed, to be the one, the only one that can serve this beautiful damsel in distress.

Beware! This is a honey trap.

She is the man-eating plant, the widow spider, the vampire bride.

She will suck you dry.

She is not a bad person, she does truly suffer, her problems are surely real and difficult to live with.

However, she doesn't have the means to have them solved.

Her whole life and identity have been created by having problems and looking for people that could help her solve them.

She has an internal mechanism that either sabotages any real possible solutions, or immediately will find other, equally unpleasant situations to suffer from.

Treat her kindly and generously. Offer to help in little things. Show her that you care and are troubled by her suffering.

However, don't let yourself be sucked into giving her any extra help or support beyond that.

Once you open up your emotional, physical or financial wallet, her needs are just so important, that she will first bleed you dry.

But then, frustrated that you haven't succeeded to solve her problems, will be angry with you for creating expectations that you haven't been able to fulfil.

Be warned, keep your distance.

4..6 The fox

The fox is charming, witty, intelligent, flattering and dangerous.

These are not bad people.

They do not wish to hurt or to harm.

They can be a real pleasure to be with.

However, a fox is a born predator, if you happen to be prey, then, I would suggest that you refuse his dinner invitation. - You might just be mistaken for the main course.

The fox, or foxy lady, will seduce you into helping them.

Working with them can be; fun, amusing, stimulating, creative, empowering, exciting, and, to begin with, a real pleasure.

However, after a certain time, and the honeymoon period can last months, even years, you will begin to notice that the quantity of work that you furnish and the amount of real benefit that you receive, is slightly, if not largely, out of balance.

On some pretext or other, the majority, if not the totality of the work will be credited to him, and all that you have put in, will count for little, if anything.

All the benefits that you succeed to reap will be on the emotional registrar, the professional rewards are for them.

So, how is brer rabbit going to avoid finishing on brer fox's dinner plate?

4.5 Brer Rabbit goes to work

So, once in that lazy south, an enterprising young fellow decided that it would be a rather interesting idea to open an office building.

All the animals were invited to come and work for the enterprise, and for this, they would get something called money.

Now money, the entrepreneur was quick to explain was a wonderful thing, for which one could exchange for all manner of interesting and amusing things.

Many of the good-natured animals agreed to go and work in the shiny metal and glass building.

And so, one cheery, sunny morning, who should come hippity-hopping into the office, but Brer Rabbit.

"How-d-y-do?" He bounced round, shaking everyone's hand.

"Good morning, Brer Rabbit. Here is your desk, you will responsible for organising and filing. When the colleagues have finished with a folder they will place it on your desk, and you will file it in one of these filing cabinets."

And he showed Brer Rabbit the rows and rows of filing cabinets.

"Do you understand?"

"Sure do, I surely, surely do." And so, the day began.

The other animals would pull out the folders, do whatever they were supposed to with them, put them on Brer Rabbit's desk, and he would file them back in the right place.

Bounce, bounce, bounce,
Open the draw and find the place,
Slip, slip, slip in the folder
Back to the desk and on with the race.

And in a hippity-huppity-hop, the morning was over and everyone stopped for a wonderful, picnic lunch, out on the finely mowed lawn, in front of the building.

"Say, Brer Rabbit, I was watching you this morning."

"Well, I wasn't watching you, Brer Fox," Brer Rabbit laughed at his bushy tailed friend.

"You sure did some impressive hop and hopping."

"Well, I be good at that."

"Yes, and you might even be the second fastest critter in this building."

"The second fastest?"

"Well, maybe you could be goin' a little faster."

"Buts I filed away all the folders that wus on my desk."

"That's just not right."

"What's 'just not right', Brer Fox?"

"That you cannot prove that you is the fastest critter working here 'cus they just aren't giving you enough things to do. Just not right."

Brer Fox continued to mutter to hisself as he walked away.

Suddenly he turns, and rushes back to Brer Rabbit.

"I got it, I got it, I got it."

"What you got Brer Fox?"

"I knows how you can prove that you is the fastest critter in the building."

"And how I do that?"

"I will share with you my work, and then you can really show just how fast you can be."

"But," he moves real close to Brer Rabbit's big, floppy ear. "You must never tell anyone, or we'll both be in a real heap of trouble."

"I swears that I won't never tell no one." And Brer Rabbit crosses his heart, his eyes and his ears. And that's a real, live-long oath.

So's that very afternoon, when no-one was looking his way, Brer Fox would slip over to Brer Rabbit's desk and add another pile of folders to put away.

And Brer Rabbit hopped faster and faster.

But as soon even before the pile on his desk started to go down, wham, another, even bigger pile appeared from no-where.

By the end of the day, he still had quite a big pile of folders on his desk when the supervisor came to see how he had done.

"Well Brer Rabbit, I've seen you hip-hopping all day long, but you're only the second fastest filing clerk is this building."

Poor Brer Rabbit, worked his butt off the whole dang day, but was still not the fastest.

'I'll show them', he said to hisself, 'I'll be the fastest tomorrow'.

But tomorrow came, and even though he almost worked hisself into the ground, he tried so hard, the supervisor just shook his head.

"Only the second fastest."

This went on all week. Faster and faster Brer Rabbit filed, and more and more Brer Fox filled his desk.

Friday came and Brer Rabbit couldn't take no more. He jus' had to know who was the filing clerk who was even faster than he was.

"Mr. Supervisor, could you please tell me, who is the filing clerk who is faster than me?"

"Why Brer Fox, he never has any folders on his desk at the end of the day."

Brer Rabbit was about to tell the supervisor about Brer Fox putting his folders on Brer Rabbit's desk, when he felt his ears crossing.

He could not tell anyone, he had taken an oath, a real, live-long oath.

Brer Fox had well and truly stuck him good, better than any sticky tar baby.

Yes um, Brer Rabbit had been well and truly trapped.

And so, Brer Rabbit went home that weekend to do some really hard thinking …

Monday morning arrives and in hops Brer Rabbit.

"How-d-y-do?" He bounces round, shaking everyone's hand.

There are already folders on his table from last week, which he cheerfully scoops up and starts to file.

Lunch time arrives and hopping and jumping he skips out onto the lawn for his picnic.

As if by accident, he bumps into Brer Bear.

"Hello Brer Rabbit, how you doin' ?"

"I'm doin' wonderfully well, thank you Brer Bear. And how are you doin' ?"

"I'm okay." Then he stops, something is tryin' to make sense in his head.

But having the sort of head that is better used to solving problems by hitting things, than by thinking things through, well, you just had to wait.

Suddenly his face lights up; his brain had managed to hitch up to something and had advanced towards an idea.

"Do you have enough folders to keep you busy?"

Brer Fox he just had to tell someone of his brilliant plan, and how he had trapped Brer Rabbit with a live-long oath to keep doing all his work for him.

And the only person that he knows well enough to share his secret with, had to be, Brer Bear.

"No, I surely do not. And if you know of any way that I could get even more folders to put away, I'd be mighty grateful."

"More folders?" Brer Bear was not sure that he had heard right. "You want more folders?" In his surprise, he had raised his voice.

"Sssshhhh, keep your voice down, don't want nobody to hear."

"Because it's a live-long oath?"

"Yes, I promised that I wouldn't tell anyone. "

"Okay."

"But if you swears a live-long oath, I can tell you."

And so he does.

"I needs more folders for the bonus."

"What bonus?"

"The bonus that I'm goin' to get, for each folder that I put away."

"I never heard of no bonus."

"That's because it's a secret. And you've gone and sworn a live-long oath that you ain't never goin' to tell no-one."

"Ah yeh, dat's right."

"See ya'." And off hops Brer Rabbit to enjoy his lunch.

He does not come back with the others, but relaxes in the sun and takes a long nap.

When he finally does come into work, you could be excused for thinking that he would have the very biggest of big piles of folders on his desk.

But there, you would be wrong.

Brer Rabbit's desk is empty.

So, he sits on his chair and he waits.

He puts his big feet on the desk, and he waits.

He spins his chair round, and round, and round, and he waits.

But no folders arrive.

After a while Brer Rabbit gets hisself off of his chair and strolls round to see what is happening.

This is what he sees:

As soon as one of the animals has finished with a folder, Brer Bear runs over to steal it right out of the hand of the clerk.

Then he is taking it and putting it on the big pile on Brer Fox's desk.

Brer Fox is running in all directions trying to cope with all the folders piling higher and higher on his desk.

And, with a faint smile on his lips, Brer Rabbit gives in his notice to the enterprise, and returns home to his peaceful, tidy burrow.

4.6 The Busy Beaver, Best Boy

Having a work colleague that is hard working and invested in their job, would seem to be a dream come true.

Unfortunately, as with anything in life, if the person or system has an extreme way of functioning that is going to become problematical.

Just why your work associate invests so much in their professional activity can, (as always), be multiple and varied; wanting to advance, family education and pressure, or even a 'private' relationship with someone higher up the chain, (one of my patients has the boss's wife as a co-worker).

The problems are likely to be; they work so much, so long, that you look bad if you don't perform as well, they pressure you to work more, or they guilt you out because they do much more work than you do.

As long as you have taken care not to have entered into a professional environment where you have sold yourself, mind, body and soul, then it should still be possible to find a solution to this.

The first, and most important action, as always, is to interrogate yourself as to this situation.

As long as you are convinced that you are doing the minimum, if not a little more, (it always pays to be a bit generous), then you will be in harmony with yourself on this exact point.

I specify that it is only on this particular aspect of the problem that you need to be comfortable with, the other emotional reactions are still to be dealt with.

As soon as you have clarified to yourself that you are working appropriately, then, already, any feelings on guilt will disappear.

What you employer or co-worker might expect, ceases to have any impact once you are in harmony with this.

In order of importance I feel that the next thing to confront is the safety of your job.

Ask for a meeting with your direct manager, and ask him, (I use the masculine for writing simplicity), for a feedback on your performance, with a written rapport of their findings.

(The crucial importance of having written traces of all important interactions, will be clearly discussed in the section dealing with mobbing).

If your manager asks to why you are asking for this meeting / rapport, there is no need to hide your motives; you have a colleague that works much more than you are, and you need to confirm that you are producing enough to cover their expectations of you.

The feedback can only be either, satisfactory or non-satisfactory. If they try to evade taking a clear position, remind them that, ultimately, they can, as Yoda states, 'do or don't do', which in this case, translates into sufficient or not.

If you fear that pushing him to position himself risks that he will be forced to respond in the negative, don't panic.

(Of course, if he says that all is okay, great, move on to the next part of the subject).

So, he shakes his head, and informs you that your work is not up to standard.

Your response is to demand a clear detailed explanation of what is not to his entire satisfaction.

If, at this point, he becomes particularly unclear or refuses to give you a detailed list, then you have a clear right to 'attack' him on this.

'If my work is not satisfactory, then there must be clear areas in which it is not up to standard.

If you cannot specify and quantify in what ways it is not good enough, then you have no grounds for your position and I insist that you reconsider your assessment.

As you are already quite convinced that your work is up to standard, it is the moment to confront your vision of your work, with that of his.

At this point, you need to open yourself up to the possibility that there are legitimate lacks in your work, it is an opportunity to get feedback so that you might improve.

On the other hand, if he lists things that you are not in agreement with, now is the time to confront him with your point of view of your own performance.

If he is a reasonable boss, (we have yet to begin on the subject of unreasonable bosses), he will be able to hear your version of reality, and hopefully, will reflect on his view of you and your work.

If the argument is that you are producing and / or working much less than your colleague, (your main motivation for having the interview, in the first place), then you need to respond to this.

The response is quite simple, 'I have been employed to do a job, to work so many hours, weeks per time period, to produce so much, (what-ever).

According to your assessment of my performance, I am succeeding to fulfil the conditions of my contract.

If I had a colleague that was not working enough, would you reduce your expectations and demands on my performance?

Clearly not. Hence, how I rate against another co-worker, should not enter into any reflection of my level of performance.'

Again, if the manager is at all reasonable, then this argument will persuade him to change his position.

So, as long as you have a superior who functions correctly, that part of the problem will have been dealt with.

The next part of the problem to resolve is the criticism and expectations of this busy beaver, himself.

The answer is to cover yourself with a thick coat of non-stick Teflon.

If he wants to work himself up, into a higher position, or down, into an early grave, then that is totally his choice.

It is for you, again, being in total harmony with the amount of work that you are, in reality succeeding to do.

And having confirmed that your boss is satisfied with your 'production', to not accept any form of criticism from your colleague.

"I appreciate how much you are doing, but I also have other things that are important to do." (Never bother to explain or defend your 'other things', it is none of their business).

If they don't want to let it go, just smile, excuse yourself politely, and walk away.

If they continue, just the same, reflect with them that they are interfering with your ability to work and that will just leave more work for them to do to catch up.

If they complain that they depend on your work so as to complete their own, suggest that maybe they should think to invest in something outside of their work, it would be good for them.

In no circumstances suggest or support the idea that they ask your boss to employ someone else.

However, in the possible case that you would be happy to increase your official work hours, this person can become an ally in asking your boss for more hours.

As I mentioned, higher up, I had a job where I didn't fit into the usual conditions of the place where I was working.

It also meant that I didn't work the same hours as all the other people in the office where I was working.

In fact, they worked from 8am, (it was an engineering company, which meant that they started working one hour before most British workers), they then worked until 5pm, five days a week.

I would stroll into work at 10am each morning, and would only work four days a week.

For which I got paid, (even if they had no way of confirming this), much more than most of them were paid.

Hence, I was both working outside the industry norms, coming in much later, and working only four days of five, and they saw themselves as working much more than I was.

So, how did this come to pass?

As I have already written elsewhere, there was a time when I was working with computers. I was living in Birkenhead, (near Liverpool), in the North West of England, and I was mandated to work for a few weeks for a company based near Glasgow, Scotland.

Through various happenings, after the end of the mandate, they asked me to stay on, as an independent contractor, and help them install and run a new computer network.

I thought for a while about the offer, which was very financially advantageous, but the problem was living and working so far away

I also realised that my function covered both 'front desk', training the engineers to use computers from the very basics; word processors, spread sheets, data bases, as well as their own custom programme, which I had managed to get working.

As well as trouble shooting any and every problem that might and did appear, on a regular basis.

However, I also had a back-office function, of installing, updating programmes, backing up the data, as well as writing programmes and data bases.

I realised that the constant disturbances made it almost impossible to advance with my 'back-office' tasks.

So, keeping in mind the geographic situation, I came up with the following solution.

First and foremost, I would only answer directly to the big boss, no one else would have any control on my functioning.

Hence, any agreement that was come to, would automatically be supported and validated by the 'highest authority'.

Next, I negotiated to work from 10am to 10pm each day. That way I would have 6 hours, (counting lunch), to deal with my front-desk duties, all the while, offering me, 5 clear hours to work on other projects.

Which, would then mean that I would largely have covered my official working hours in just 4 days, leaving me the possibility to drive home to my family late on Thursday night or Friday, during the day, depending on my level of fatigue.

So, first, I was clear on the reasonableness of this organisation, hence, no problem of guilt.

Secondly, this deal was negotiated and agreed by my boss, (the big boss), therefore neutralising any questions about my working schedule.

Finally, as to the other workers. Some, I would bother to mention that I would still be working until 10pm, some I wouldn't even bother to inform.

Some believed me, some didn't.

Clearly, those people that mattered to me, they fully understood and appreciated why I had organised myself in this fashion, and supported me in my planning.

Those that chose to not believe me, and thought that I was a cheat and an abuser, I chose to ignore and continue my life.

This deal lasted a full year, and it was a great and enriching experience for me, and I trust that I was satisfactory to all those that I worked with and for.

(I never heard anything to the contrary. My contract was terminated by the 'mother' company that owned the company that I worked for.

And I believe that my network was finally integrated into the general computer system of that mother company).

5. Your Boss

Most bosses, being human beings, and subject to pressures, either from their own bosses, or from the outside world, if they are their own bosses, can be difficult at times.

As in any relationship, we need to accept that the other can be; unpleasant, unhelpful, under-appreciative or a total pain in the arse, that's just life.

In these cases, when the outside problem has been resolved, they can then return to their 'normal' state, which one would expect to be fairly reasonable

Unfortunately, not all bosses have a normal state that is easy to cope with, and it is these types of people that we need to think of how to deal with.

5.1 Some Thoughts on Evil Bosses

Before I launch into list of abusive bosses, it is important to remember that our behaviours are learned and integrated from an early age.

No matter how unpleasant, violent, manipulative or abusive these people might be, they rarely see themselves in that light.

Each one tries to do their best, living up to the values and obligations that they have been trained into.

They rarely intend to hurt or abuse, they just do what seems right and defendable to themselves.

An abuser is always an ancient abused.

This, in no way gives them the right to abuse others, and everyone has the right and obligation to protect themselves.

However, some of the personality types and behaviours that I am about to describe below can seem particularly unpleasant.

They often could even enter into the realm of psychiatric illness.

The aim of this book is not to vilify certain of your employers.

The aim is to help you to take the necessary distance, so as to be able perceive their modes of functioning.

And hence, to be able to find the most appropriate action, so as to find your most successful path in the work environment.

And remember, the 'final argument of kings', to attack and destroy, is rarely successful.

Rather, follow the opposing adage, 'he who fights and runs away, lives to fight, another day', to leave, can sometimes be the only long-term solution.

5.2 Jekyll and Hyde
Friend and Foe

The Jekyll and Hyde boss, as one can imagine can be rather changeable.

However, it is not they are sometimes and nice and sometimes particularly unpleasant that sets them apart.

There are many, many of us that are sensitive, changeable, or reactive some-times or other.

What characteristic differentiates these from the rest of humanity is the clear dichotomy between their moments of clear and exaggerated friendliness and caring, and a cold, nasty even vindictive attitude.

These are the bosses that hunt you out, seduce you into their work domain, invite to their homes, introduce you to their families, make you feel that you are truly one of their special friends.

Only to suddenly find yourself confronted with their evil doppelganger!

Unavailable, irritable, unreasonable, uncaring.

However, the minute that you express your unhappiness with them. They are equally capable to continue to be the scary twin, ready to insult and aggress you, as they are capable to transform into your best friend, and re-seduce you into accepting your conditions, as 'we are all in this together, and you are so much appreciated.'

This is especially prevalent in small, family run businesses, where the owner knows each of his employees by name, and can play the friendship card, at any moment.

I've known employees that worked masses of overtime, even accepted pay cuts, just to keep the business functioning.

Either this goes on indefinitely, with no clear resolution, but never a total transparency of the finances.

Which means that the owner still succeeds to hold onto his comfortable lifestyle, (possibly keeping his usual salary).

Or

Things improve and things go back to, 'business as usual'.

However, after the crises is over, and the company is back in the black, there is very rarely any real acknowledgment from the management or owner, of the sacrifices made by the employees, nor any tangible form of appreciation.

So, what is best way to deal with type of situation?

Strangely enough, by using his own functioning against himself.

His image of himself is most likely to be of the nice guy; friendly, caring, generous, and a good person all round.

It is only the difficult circumstances that force him to act the way that he has to.

Hence, to demand to see him and inform him that the circumstances that you are finding yourself in, even if you have accepted them up until now, are unacceptable, and that they must change.

Yes, there is always the danger that Mr. Hyde will unsheathe his hidden dagger and rip your throat out, (it's the chance that one must take).

However, there seems to me, to be as much chance, if not more than likely, that the Jekyll part will, sooner or later surface, and you will get a reasonable response.

5.3 Trumping Mr. Hyde with Dr Jekyll.

In one of my places of employment, (you might guess which one), I was in this exact situation.

The employer was regularly complaining about not having enough money. He was clearly a total spend-thrift, spending money left, right and centre.

I had been promised, over some weeks that my unpaid trainee position would be transformed into one where I would get some payment.

The same week that I was due to have this important discussion with my boss, I was called into the general office by his administrative assistant, and informed that there wasn't enough money for me to get paid – anything!!

By miracle, my boss was free at that moment.

I stormed into his office, and confronted him with the total unfairness of the situation.

We then had a shouting match in his office, with, at the end, my threatening to leave.

He warned me that if I left his office in that moment, then there would be no turning back.

So, controlling my anger, I asked him what he would propose.

He answered that he would confer with his assistant and get back to me before the end of the day.

In any other world, I would have been fired on the spot.

Good to his word, before the end of the day, he had a deal for me.

Although still rather abusive, it was good enough for me to accept, and life carried on, strangely enough, totally as usual.

It was only after the 2nd shouting match with him that he decided that, enough was enough.

However, even then, he didn't fire me, he organised for me to go and work with another colleague of his.

Another, totally unlikely, but absolutely true story.

5.4 The Vampire

This is one of the classic, abusive boss types.

She, (why not a she, for this time?), she sucks all your energy, ideas and creativity for herself.

This was the premise for the wonderful 'Working Girl' film, and we see it on a regular basis both in fiction, as in real life.

No matter what you succeed to do, to create, she will find a way to package and to sell it as her own work.

Whether she is friendly, kind and supportive, or nasty, demanding and openly abusive, the outcome is always the same, everything of value that you produce is her work.

She might succeed to convince you that you are a team and that whatever success she might have, you will benefit from it. That if these ideas were presented by you and not her, then they would not be taken seriously.

Don't think that you might simply let those people higher know up that this is the fruit of your efforts, she is also the queen of blocking any access that her subordinates might have to her associates and superiors.

So, what to do?

Clearly, the most honest and healthy approach is to try and talk openly to her about how you are feeling that she does little to advance your reputation within the company, and that, that is a problem for you.

If, by miracle this works, then go to the end of this section, do not pass 'go', but treat yourself, (and a friend), to a really great meal!!

On the other hand, if this only ends in her promising you some vague assurances that you will have your validation, but not quite yet, or something similar, then you have but three options:

Accept that things are as they are, maybe they will change, but you can wait.

Look for another job, either in the same enterprise, or elsewhere.
Choose to fight.

The first two choices need no further reflection, however, the third would entail a risky and complicated strategy.

Before you read further, if this really is your reality, ask yourself if you are prepared to follow the value systems of Machiavelli's 'Dark Prince' and of Wáng Jīngzé's 36 Stratagems.

Be sure that you are totally in harmony with lying and manipulating to 'win this battle'.

This is not the type of technique that I would generally suggest. However, if you are genuinely convinced that your self-esteem will not allow to act otherwise, and you are willing to risk all, 'on one game of pitch and toss', (again, 'If' by Kipling), then I have something to suggest.

You are sure that for you, 'the end justifies the means'? (Machiavelli), then read on …

5.5 Staking out the Vampire

To outmanoeuvre this boss, will take daring and planning.

First, follow on from your direct demand to have your name advanced with your work, by reflecting, that she is the only person that knows of the quality of your efforts.

Hence, if something would happen to her, everything that you have done for her would count for nothing if you needed to look for another job, (or even protect the one that you have.)

At least, she could write you an interim work report, stating that you were a willing and dedicated collaborator, who is creative and invested in his work.

If she refuses even this, then it is truly a lost cause, - give up. (Retreat is the last, and the safest of the 36 stratagems).

If you can get this document, then the next step is to get the email addresses of all the important people that your boss works with.

You might already have them, or you might need to find a way to get her to forward to you a circular message that includes all their names.

A simple strategy might just be to ask her BCC you for an email that describes a project that you are working on, where you would do well to be kept informed.

These next steps will take patience and perseverance.

Once you safely have these precious addresses, it is time to approach step 3.

Now you have to choose a very important project that you are doing most of the work for.

Carefully construct a historic of each step that you have taken by keeping your boss, up-to-date on your progress.

Send the email to her, but also bcc to your private email address, and if, at all possible, to someone of confidence in your organisation.

(Yes, this might seem paranoid, but you will only get one shot of this, so aim to protect yourself on every level).

- If it feels like you are reading a plot for a film, don't worry, it might end up being one.

However, don't let her know where you really are with the project, let her think that you are less advanced than in reality.

Allow the deadline for the meeting to advance, and as she starts to pressure you to work quicker, start to complain about tiredness, eyestrain, headaches, and the like.

Warning! If you are not an Oscar nominated actor, do NOT overplay this, better play it right down, and take the risk that it is too weak, rather than too strong.

Be sure that other people that you work with know that you are not doing well.

Just drop the occasional remark, if they don't react, let it go. They will still likely remember this later.

Allow her to start to panic, show that you are working, as best that you can, but don't let her realise that you have nearly finished the project.

The day before the presentation, call in sick.

Say that you have taken the project home with you, and even though you are sick, that you will do the best that you can to finish it before the presentation.

On the day of the presentation, send all your work to all the people on your list of important executives, but not her. Excusing yourself for not having it ready earlier, and so you have thought to send it directly to them, to be sure that they have a copy before this meeting.

Hopefully, she will have worked through the night to have something to show to her colleagues, that will not be as good as your work.

This is the moment in the film where the chief executive confronts her and asks who you are and why they didn't know that you even existed.

She tries to lie and say that it was always all her own work and that you just 'helped out', and then you appear with all the email proof that, that is another lie, and you then marry the top executive, and live happily ever after.

Of course, it is unlikely to happen like this, but it might get you past the secretary and door of one of the executives, so that you can expose the situation and ask to have a boss that will openly support you in your work.

If she tries to fire you, 'on the spot', then, in most countries, you could file for unfair dismissal, and send a recommended letter to the executives and the human resources department.

You explain the situation, saying that you, from your sick bed, were only trying to help and that you sent the emails in good faith.

That she has sacked you purely because she was embarrassed that other people found out that she was stealing your work, and to prove that, that is true, that she has recently written you a glowing interim rapport.

Would something like this work, or is it just the fantasy of a frustrated writer?

I wouldn't know, but it would be an interesting stratagem to try out.

5.6 The Invisible Man

The invisible man, is a sort of latter day Scarlet Pimpernel. And for those of you too young to have heard of this personage, he was the brave persona of the openly effeminate Percy Blakeney, who was wont to quote:
"They seek him here, they seek him there,
Those Frenchies seek him everywhere.
Is he in heaven? Or is he in hell?
That damned elusive Pimpernel!" (Scarlet Pimpernel [1934])

Well, our boss, the invisible man, is a bit of the same.

Every time that there is an important; decision to be taken, every time a necessary piece of work needs to be checked, every time a difficult client phones up, he damn well disappears.

And yet, whenever there is something interesting to do, or to present, 'hey presto', he pulls himself, magically, out of his own hat. (Please feel totally free to exchange 'hat' for your own, more colourful adjective).

Of course, any movement on your behalf to find any alternative to his making decisions or prechecking important documents is strongly blocked, and he clearly reminds you of the hierarchy and your lowly position in it.

However, his unavailability needs not be such an obstacle.

Do not worry if he is not around when you need him.

Just send him a message, better an email, with his boss in CC, explaining that there is decision that needs to be taken by whatever time and date.

If you do not feel capable to take the decision, then do nothing, and just duck when the excrement hits the fan.

Or, if you do feel capable, take the decision and again email your and his boss, informing them of the fact that you felt obliged to act as you did, and you hope that they are okay with your choice.

This is likely to have one of three outcomes:

1.   Your boss succeeds to get you fired. (Sorry, bad call)
2.   Your boss becomes more available
3.   You get an explicit or implicit right to make decisions in your boss's place.

In every case, you are no longer in that difficult situation.

5.7 Napoleon

Having a Napoleonic boss is not the worst-case scenario, but it can be challenging to find a healthy balance.

Basically, Napoleons, as with their namesake, want to conquer the planet.

You are a solder in their army. They might or might not express their need and appreciation of you. In either case there are pluses and minuses; on the plus side of being noticed, we feel special and more motivated to make even more efforts, otherwise, we might be even more motivated to work hard enough to be seen.

Elon Musk; the founder, CEO, and CTO of SpaceX; CEO, and product architect of Tesla Inc.; as of May 2017, who has an estimated net worth of $15.2 billion,[4] is one of the most famous Napoleons of our time.

---

[4] Wikipedia, https://en.wikipedia.org/wiki/Elon_Musk, retrieved 21 06 2017

He is an incredibly hard worker, brilliant and strongly motivational. Those that work with him express a guru type of devotion to the man and his projects.

To be in direct contact with such a demi-god must be an extremely privileged experience.

However, the costs of such an association can be exceptionally high in; time, energy, health and relationship.

There is almost a sect consciousness, with the mantra being, 'we can do it'.

Again, I repeat, the experience can be life changing, highly rewarding, even ecstatic, (in the largest sense of the term).

So, how to assure that one has the right life balance?

Every once in a while, I would suggest, at least twice per year. Take yourself away from this environment, (it doesn't have to be a regular job, it could be a political cause, social work, or any other group situation).

Isolate yourself from that group, and check up on your current life priorities.

The simplest way to do this is to write yourself some lists.

1.　What am I gaining from my commitment?
2.　What is the cost for which I am paying for this gain?
3.　How important are these costs and benefits for me, at this time?
4.　What other life needs, wishes and desires, are not being fulfilled?
5.　What would be the costs in my commitment to my group be, if I moved some of my resources from the group, to invest in these other benefits?
6.　How important are these costs and benefits for me, at this time?

Remembering that the basic tenant of these books is, 'being in harmony with oneself', take the time and distance to quietly and coolly assess your answers to these questions.

If your appreciation of your current investment, is that you are globally happy with the deal, then great. Keep on truckin' !

If you realise that your Napoleon is taking off of you much more than you are gaining, then it seems clear that it must be time to look elsewhere, and to move on.

Unfortunately, things in life are rarely that cut and dried.

More than likely, the costs and benefits of staying in the group, and those of leaving it, don't give a totally clear indication of what is right for you.

In this case, what might be a short-term response, would be, to change nothing, but keep a more focused attention on the costs and benefits of continuing, and wait until the net review moment, before acting.

If that doesn't seem reasonable, or you have done the exercise and have again found yourself at this unclear place, then another strategy might be worth reflecting on.

How might I fantasise to change my investment, imagining that I had the power to choose exactly how much time and energy, I would wish to invest, so as to have the optimum cost – benefit from my 'work'?

Do NOT allow yourself to question the possibility of the reaction of the boss or others in the group, of your desired changes. It is paramount, that you give yourself total freedom to imagine a best-case scenario for yourself.

In therapy, we sometimes suggest that the patient has a magic ward, and that he can change anything in his life, anything that could improve his well-being.

You need to be in the same state of mind.

Once you have fantasised, your optimum level or type of investment in your group, then you can start to question as to how you might implement it.

Strangely enough, in this type of situation, we all too often find, to everyone's great surprise, that the institution is quite open to find a working compromise.

The reason for this, is that these groups are formed around an ideal, or more exactly an idol.

They rarely need to create restrictive practices or rigid rules. The desire of the group members to participate, is generally enough to keep them functioning at an optimal level.

Hence, if you ask for different arrangement, the administration is often quite flexible in their response.

However, what might be more difficult to handle is the reaction of the other group members, and it is even possible that, sooner or later, you might be excluded, by them, from your 'sect'.

Whether or not this happens, is very much dependant on how you handle the situation from your side, and the importance of the sect consciousness of the group members.

Depending on whether you succeed to make this work or not, will give you your answer whether to continue or not.

5.8 The Great and Powerful Oz
(The Narcissist)

"I am Oz, the great and powerful", so sayeth the Wizard of Oz, hiding behind his curtain of flames, with his enormous head projected above it.

The narcissist is a very dangerous creature, their need to be seen as; powerful / wonderful / creative / successful, makes them capable to destroy anyone that threatens these needs.

At their most extreme, they might even be considered to have a psychiatrically defined narcissistic personality disorder, (NPD).

According to the ***DSM-5***, individuals with NPD have most or all of the following symptoms, typically without commensurate qualities or accomplishments.

- Grandiosity with expectations of superior treatment from others
- Fixated on fantasies of power, success, intelligence, attractiveness, etc.

- Self-perception of being unique, superior and associated with high-status people and institutions
- Needing constant admiration from others
- Sense of entitlement to special treatment and obedience from others
- Exploitative of others to achieve personal gain
- Unwilling to empathize with others' feelings, wishes, or needs
- Intensely envious of others and the belief that others are equally envious of them
- Pompous and arrogant demeanour.

As with all things in life, people's personality traits exist on a continuum, and one can find that all managers are somewhere between having fairly high self-esteem and NPD.

Clearly, the cases that we are looking at here, are those that find themselves towards the top end of the scale.

If you have a manager that scores high on at least five of these personality traits, they will need to be dealt with in a rather careful manner.

The DSM specifies that these people have the ***symptoms typically without commensurate qualities or accomplishments,*** however, many very successful people have these traits, but do have commensurate qualities or accomplishments.

And, fairly often, we find managers, bosses and owners, that are clearly narcissistic, yet can be intelligent, well-educated / well-trained, seductive, hard-working, creative and hence, worthy of the successes that they have.

That doesn't change the fact that they still have strong narcissistic tendencies, and that will make them potentially difficult to work for.

Strangely enough, narcissistic bosses are not the worst bosses in the world.

True, they need to get the most and the best.

Yes, they look for constant appreciation and validation.

And, they can be very controlling and manipulative.

However, if you do not threaten them, moreover, if they find you helpful and supportive of their needs for positive recognition, they can be most generous.

You can even challenge them, argue with them, to a point. The point is, at the end, you always allow them to win.

To return to my history with my psychiatrist boss, who admittedly had certain narcissistic traits, even though I dared to have two major rows with him, I (consciously and intentionally), backed down, and gave up to him, in the end.

This was a total strategic necessity, if I hadn't, I would have been thrown out immediately, but because I did, he chose to give me what I demanded.

He was also not against inviting us to support him and participate in courses that he was giving, or even conferences and groups that he was animating.

5.9 The Donkey and the Cock

Once there was a farm, and separating the farmyard from the main buildings was a gorgeous, green, high hedge.

Every morning, the animals would gather, in front of the hedge to marvel at the daily show, put on by the cock.

He would, sing, dance, jump and slide, there and back, along the length of the hedge.

Even, when he seemed to not be making any effort to move, he could still be seen, gliding left and right.

What none of the other animals were aware of, was that the cock, succeeded this surprising feat, by conducting his performance, while perched on the head of the donkey.

And it was the donkey, walking, even trotting, there and back, behind the hedge that made the performance so extraordinary.

All went quite well until the day the donkey got talking to the pig.

"He's just using you to look good. What do you get out of all this, other than a sore neck?"

The donkey reflected on this for a while.

"Why is it always you sitting and dancing on my head, and not the other way around?"

"Because I am the cock, and you are the donkey."

"Well I've had enough, I'm not doing this anymore."

"As you wish."

And the two of them parted their ways.

The next day, the cock was back singing and dancing on the hedge. Although the movements weren't quite as fast, nor as smooth as before, the show still went on.

The donkey, intrigued, went to look behind the scene, only to find that the 'supporting act', was Ethel the Cow.

Later that day, the Donkey crossed the Cock, on his way to the barn.

"It's not as good with Ethel," he remarked in passing.

"True, true, you are much better than she is."

"Then why would you let me leave?"

"Because you do what you want."

"I just want some appreciation."

"Well I appreciate you, you boost me up, and help me look good."

"But I need for the others to see me, to know that I am there."

"Fine, I'll expect you tomorrow morning as usual." And with that, he strolled off to the hen house.

The next morning, everything passed as usual, and the Donkey was starting to think that the Cock had just tricked him.

When, right at the end of the performance, the Cock directed him past the end of the hedge, and then round back into the yard.

"Just in case you might be wondering how I perform my wonderful act, here is my faithful support, Mr. Donkey."

He then jumped off of the donkey's head.

"Take a bow Mr. Donkey, thanks to you, I am the greatest cock in all the county."

5.10 The Marquis de Sade
The Master of Mobbing

So, finally we arrive at the most problematic of situations, mobbing.

The sadistic boss seems to find more pleasure in finding a weak colleague to abuse, then advancing with all their other work.

This is unlikely to be totally true, but they still seem to relish each opportunity to aggress and abuse certain people that they have under their power.

Yes, there are also fellow workers, on the same level as ourselves, that seem to be able to make our lives a misery.

These are usually well protected by the hierarchy, but they are still less dangerous and problematical then our sadistic superiors.

Whether they are into public humiliation for minor errors or prefer to rip your self-confidence into shreds with demining and destructive notes and emails, the effect is eventually the same.

You begin to fear going into work.

And yet you lack the courage to leave. Whether that is because your self-image has been so tarnished that you cannot even imagine presenting for another job, or that you fear that any future employer will contact this boss, and after the awful things that he would say, any chance of being employed is close to zero.

Of course, you have already tried to reason with him.

And you've already contacted the human resources department. Unfortunately, he has already gotten there first, and they consider you as a lazy, difficult, disruptive, employee. So, they have little time to listen to your complaints.

Suicide, either personal or professional starts to become more and more attractive, but you are not quite ready to give up quite yet.

You are aware that you are in a much weaker position than him, he has much more force than you do.

So, how might one possibly succeed in such a situation?

5.11 Some theoretical concepts

Imagine that you and your opponent will be facing each other in a fight, but you have the choice of which discipline you will be using.

The two types of fighting where you are the most disadvantaged would be boxing and karate, where physical strength and force give him the greatest advantage.

However, what if you were to choose Aikido or Judo? Judo and Aikido use the opponents own strength and force against them. Here, having a strong, powerful attacker is not a problem, you just have to learn the right techniques, and to be quick and smart to win.

In your work situation, you are faced with a much more powerful opponent. You need to use patience and perseverance, teamed with subtlety and strategy to overcome him.

Before continuing, I'd like to take a moment to talk about Aikido, and some of its principles.

Stefan Stenudd in his excellent book, Aikido Principles, Basic Concepts of the Peaceful Martial Art, delves into this 'impossible martial art'.

He explains that the creation of term Aikido comes from; Ai – harmony, Ki – life energy and Do – the way.

And that 'most of the aikido characteristics happen to be negations: In aikido there is no competition, no attack techniques, no opponent, no force needed, no shortcut possible.'[5]

---

[5]Aikido Principles, Basic Concepts of the Peaceful Martial Art

by Stefan Stenudd, Arriba Publ., 2008, 2016, ISBN: 978-1-5331-4237-5

Turning now to the theory and practice of judo. Looking on the Online Dojo net site, under Judo Info[6]

Some Basic Judo Principles:

" Judo techniques enable a weak and small man to overcome a large and strong man because they are based on scientific principles such as leverage and balance.

The first thing to learn is never to oppose strength to strength. If you do that the stronger man will inevitably win.

Remember that when he is on balance he is strong, but off balance he is weak, providing you have retained your own balance to take advantage of his weakness.

---

[6] http://judoinfo.com/unbalance/
retrieved the 07.07.2017

The second principle you should understand and think about is the action of levers. You know how much easier it is to lift a heavy object by putting a crowbar under it.

If you rest the end on the ground, have the object a little way up the lever, and lift the other end of the bar, you are using your crowbar as a lever of the second class.

It is important to throw your opponent by making use of his loss of balance.

If you want to make him fall, you make him lose his balance; that is, you cause his center of gravity to go outside the base. Then the gravity that acts on him works for you to make him lean or fall.

The Aims of Practice

From the brief statement of principles above, it will be seen that the immediate aims of practice are three-fold:

1. To learn the techniques.
2. To learn non-resistance, so that the opponent can be made to put himself off balance.
3. To develop speed and timing in the application of the techniques."

Although we need to defend ourselves from this perverted, prince of darkness, we also need to protect ourselves from 'spiritual contamination'.

We have already tried to reason with him, and we are aware that someone that abuses others, has surely been abused in the past and continues to suffer in the present from that abuse.

However, their inability or lack of desire to control or treat their own emotional pain, certainly does not give them the right to inflict this on others.

And yet, we must not let ourselves descend to his level, if he is to be depowered, damaged, even destroyed, it has to be by his own hand.

We need to allow him, himself to damage his own position and reputation. That way, our hands are clean, we can still look at ourselves in the mirror and see someone moral, honest, spiritual.

Often, in my sessions, I use the image of the of the game of curling.

For those of you not clear on what curing is: "Curling is a sport in which players slide stones on a sheet of ice towards a target area which is segmented into four concentric circles…. The curler can induce a curved path by causing the stone to slowly turn as it slides, and the path of the rock may be further influenced by two sweepers with brooms who accompany it as it slides down the sheet, using the brooms to alter the state of the ice in front of the stone."[7]

---

[7] https://en.wikipedia.org/wiki/Curling retrieved the 07.07.2017

And what is 'sweeping'?

In Curl Tech's, 'The Curling Manual'[8] In their Section 6 – Sweeping, they explain that:

"The sweeping motion briefly polishes the ice (pebble) just before the rock travels over it. The sweeping action melts a molecular layer of ice for a very brief moment, resulting in a molecular layer of water. This creates an even lower friction environment that helps the naturally occurring frictional melting. This combination allows the rock to decelerate slower. This results in the rock traveling farther.

The technical definition of sweeping is that it decreases the rate of deceleration. The overall reduction in friction has another effect: Since the rock is dragging less on both sides, the rock will travel straighter."

8

http://www.curlingschool.com/manual2007/Section6.html   retrieved 07.07.2017

So, what, (you might well ask), has got to do with anything?

Sweeping, is the image that I use when I am talking about, what is now termed, 'Enabling'.

Enabling is supporting someone to do something, or continue to do something. A behaviour, which without this support, might slow down or become extinguished.

It can either be helpful, if the attitude or act is positive for the person, or most destructive if this conduct is, in itself detrimental. The most often detrimental conduct sited, is that of alcoholism.

Elina Kala, MA, writing on the Betty Ford website, [9] states that:

---

[9] http://www.hazeldenbettyford.org/articles/kala/enabling-fact-sheet   APRIL 6, 2016 | BY: Elina Kala, MA,

Mental Health Professional

Retrieved 07.07.2017

"Enabling behavior, simply put, shields people from experiencing the full impact and consequences of their behavior. Enabling is different from helping and supporting in that it allows the enabled person to be irresponsible."

Returning to the image of sweeping:

By removing the natural friction and resistance, we facilitate a movement to continue further and longer than it would otherwise.

However, as these behaviours, are also motivated by a desire to continue, this gives the 'ice', a slight downward angle. If most friction and resistance is removed, not only can, in these instances, the 'rock' continues to advance, it can even increase its speed and the force of this direction.

Hence, just as with the curling puck, by sweeping or enabling, we become able to influence both the speed and the direction of the object, of the person.

5.12 Kill with a borrowed sword

(借刀殺人／借刀杀人, Jiè dāo shā rén)

In the 36 stratagems, the 'Kill with a borrowed sword', is an excellent way to win over a stronger foe.

"Attack using the strength of another (in a situation where using one's own strength is not favourable). Trick an ally into attacking him, bribe an official to turn traitor, or *use the enemy's own strength against him.* The idea here is to cause damage to the enemy by getting a third party to do the deed." [10]

So how do we apply these elements so as to neutralise, even rebound the negative functioning of this type of boss?

The first step is to remove yourself emotionally from being a target.

---

[10] Wikipedia The 36 Stratagems
https://en.wikipedia.org/wiki/Thirty-Six_Stratagems retrieved the 06 07 2017

What does that mean?

It means that every action, word, look or other, that has, up until now been experienced as an attack on you as a worker, as a person, now needs to be experienced as an opportunity to draw your boss into losing his balance.

You cease to be a real target and become a perceived target.

The Borg, in the Star Trek series, often repeat that, 'resistance is futile', in this case, it is not only futile, but painful.

The concept is easy enough to understand; if someone strong goes to punch you, and you block them, the chances are high, that even if you succeed to block them correctly, it will still hurt.

On the other hand, if you move out of the way, then there can be no contact, hence no pain.

But, you might reflect, in a territorial war you will lose ground. Here, I must remind you of Napoleon's disastrous campaign against the Russians, where he lost about ninety percent of his forces, but only fought two real battles, and yet he succeeded to enter into St. Petersburg.

Ceding ground, does not mean losing the war.

The technique is to convince yourself that every attack, on any level is only offering you more and more ammunition to be shot back towards him. As if he is throwing boomerangs at a mirage of you, that will, sooner or later, return to him, in a way that he will not be able to catch them, only be struck by his own missiles.

Remember the Aikido position; :
'In aikido there is no competition, no attack techniques, no opponent, no force needed.'

Judo; 'To learn non-resistance, so that the opponent can be made to put himself off balance.'

Curling; By removing the natural friction and resistance, we facilitate a movement to continue further and longer than it would otherwise

Enabling; 'Enabling is different from helping and supporting in that it allows the enabled person to be irresponsible.'

By your position of none reaction, non-resistance, this will only excite him act more.

In my experience of working with people that have been mobbed, to begin with, the mobber tends to be quite careful, using subtle attacks or orchestrating or benefitting from real situations where the inferior might legitimately be criticised.

What often then happens is that the 'mobbee' then reacts inappropriately, in some way, either to defend themselves, or to express their pain and suffering, only giving more and more excuses to be attacked.

To look at it in a martial arts context; the attacker connects with his foe, that percussion, then throws the person off balance, thereby allowing the attacker more and more opportunities to continue to subdue their opponent.

By offering a false target, your assailant will attack, not connect, become more and more frustrated, start to make mistakes, and leave himself 'open to the kill'.

The image of the matador comes to mind; he offers the bull the red cloth as part of himself, as the target. The bull charges, and he adjusts the cloth so that he is no longer behind it.

The bull attacks the cloth, which harms not the matador, further and further frustrating the bull.

By not resisting, what I do not mean is to accept each and every criticism that is thrown at you. Certainly not.

By not resisting, we mean not to enter into any type of conflict.

So how does this work?

Every time that there is any sort of criticism of you, respond, as honestly as you can, in written, (always in written, there must be a physical trace of all interactions), your response to these accusations.

Explaining, clearly and fully why things have happened as they have, all and any past discussions that you might have had, when you have drawn his attention to dysfunctions in any of the work systems, especially those due to him.

The tone needs to be always, positive, polite and constructive.

These documents need to be regularly printed out and might eventually constitute a legal dossier.

One that could be presented to the HR department, his boss, his boss's boss, (especially if he has a protective relationship with his direct boss), a sympathetic manager from another department, (remember, Kill with a borrowed sword), or even some outside legal structure.

Once you integrate the concept that every time that he attacks you, this will add more damning evidence against him, instead of running away from the bull, it becomes much more interesting to wander around the centre of the arena, offering yourself as an appetizing target.

But that is not all.

This new attitude of yours of not showing that his 'slings and arrows', are having any effect, will have one of two consequences; either he will give up on you as a 'catspaw' and find another, more entertaining victim, or else he will 'raise the temperature'.

Upping the heat, will mean that he will look for more and more excuses to attack you.

As long as you are working as best as you can, being polite and helpful, he will have to search further and further out of the shadows, to find something to attack you with.

By being the best worker that you can be, you are sweeping the ice in front of him. He expects that when he pushes you, you will push back, he needs for you to resist. By not giving him this resistance, you are enabling him to push further and further.

By backing away from any direct conflict, he will have to stretch further and further out.

As he stretches further, he becomes more and more unbalanced, more and more and more venerable.

Now comes the question, when to go for the 'coup de grâce'?

If you are convoked for a disciplinary hearing, or worst still, fired, then you have little choice when to react.

If you have no strict timing, it is usually a good idea to wait until you have just had an annual work assessment, or if that doesn't exist in your work environment, try your best to get some sort of assessment document before you act.

If the assessment is positive, that will support your position against your boss's treatment of you, if it is unreasonably negative, it will also support your position.

From there, with or without already consulting your union or an employment lawyer, you can choose to demand a meeting with your boss, and / or ; someone from your HR, his boss, your boss's boss and present them with a copy of your printed dossier, insisting that this behaviour ceases, or else you will take matters further.

What 'taking matters further', will mean, depends very much on your own specific circumstances.

However, it must not be ignored that there is a real risk that you might lose your job because of this, and be ready to assume this eventuality.

Many of my patients were so fed up with this that they often took this risk, although, most of them were satisfied with the outcome. (We have a very strong anti-mobbing culture in Switzerland).

In any case the situation will likely get resolved and you will be able to look yourself in the mirror, knowing that you have, at some level succeeded to win against a work bully.

6. Your Subordinates

6.1 It's good to be king

So, finally you've made it. You've been promoted, you are now a manager.
Great!

Well, not really. There are almost as many hurdles and pot-holes for managers as there are for those at the bottom of the ladder.

There are two basic situations in which you might find yourself; either you are promoted within the office, workplace where you have already been working and you know and are known by everyone, or else, you enter into a new environment where everything is an unknown.

The pluses of continuing in the same workplace are; you know everyone, they know you, you know how things function, and you might already have some ideas of how to improve things.

The downsides are; you might have been indoctrinated into accepting certain inefficient customs and practices, your colleagues might resist accepting you as their boss.

On the other hand, arriving in a new office; gives a new perspective to the job, you and your new colleagues can discover each other, with you in this role, you can have a neutral regard on the systems and habits.

But, you will need to learn how things are, how they work, who are your subordinates, their strengths and weaknesses, become part of that system, and install changes where necessary.

To look quickly at the two scenarios.

Being promoted in the same workplace involves a change in your professional relationships.

I would suggest that you call a meeting of all your colleagues to clarify your new role and responsibilities.

Explaining that you are here to guarantee the correct and best functioning of this department and the best conditions for everybody concerned.

However, you have to respond to the demands of upper management, (or whatever), and that means that you might have to criticise some people and help them to help the team to achieve the required targets.

From there on in, it is your own management style that will direct how you continue to function in the team.

When facing a totally new, (there can of course be in-betweens), workspace it is important to enter correctly into this new world.

The three steps that I mentioned at the beginning, when entering into a new team; (observation, imitation, integration), should be followed. However, as a manager, there will be a fourth step; re-creation.

After you have taken the time to enter, seeing how things function, who the other actors are, and allowing them the time to get to know you, then comes the step to impose your vision and your own procedures.

As a manager, especially if you lack much experience in this function, I would suggest that you integrate, what I term as the 'Indian P's', (no not peas!).

Having spent a little time in India, I have noted that a certain section of the population, are not as quick to respond to requests, as I might wish.

I go, I ask, they smile, make that special, 'maybe yes', type of nod of the head, I leave, naively expecting something to happen, and I wait, and I wait, and I wait.

After a certain length of time, I return, and the game starts a new round.

Unfortunately, certain types of reactions; being angry, expressing impatience, being cynical, being too timid, or ultimately, giving up, do not facilitate a successful outcome.

What, through a certain amount of experience, I discovered works best, are what I have termed the Indian P's; Patience, Persistence, Politeness, Precision, and Pleasantness.

When dealing with most people, especially from a position of authority.

I you follow the P's, there is a most high probability that you will succeed to get what you wish for without losing any hair.

Another important subject to reflect on is that of power, responsibility and letting go.

Responsibility and power must be partners. As a manager, you will have a list of responsibilities, which your superiors will charge you with fulfilling.

As long as they give you the necessary power to make the decisions necessary, then all will be fine, (hopefully).

However, if they insist on your succeeding their targets, but will not offer you the means that you feel that you need to carry out these orders, then you might find yourself in an impossible position.

The answer, in such a situation, is to choose to 'let go'.

Do not allow yourself to be railroaded into attempting the impossible, and finishing in failure.

I once had a patient who was put under pressure to fulfil certain targets, but was not given the necessary resources to succeed.

He would go to his boss complaining that he didn't know to make it work with the means that he had.

The boss's response was; "If I have to find the answer to your problems, what are you being paid for?" And would throw him out of the office.

I reflected with my patient that he was there to solve the problems of his subordinates, for which he was being paid.

His boss was there to solve my patient's problems, and that is why the boss was being paid.

If you do not have the means to make it work, do not try and force your team to regularly do the impossible, you will then become the manager from Hell.

Also, when you ascend towards the status of manager, you will also need to accept to delegate tasks that you might, hitherto have undertaken yourself.

This, from my own experience can be problematical, especially if you do not have one hundred percent confidence in your collaborator.

"It is smal reason you should kepe a dog, and barke your selfe." So wrote Brian Melbancke in his novel "Philotimus: the Warre Betwixt Nature and Fortune", 1583[11]

'Don't keep a dog and bark yourself', or don't pay someone to do a task, and then do it yourself.

The reason that we have other people in our team, is so that you can delegate tasks to them, while you get on with other things.

If you know these tasks well, great, you are excellently well placed to check that the person is doing their job correctly. Only, remember, it is now their job, and they might do it; better, worse and / or differently than you.

As long as the job is reasonably well done, then that has to be okay. You have many other and more important tasks to do.

---

[11] http://www.phrases.org.uk/meanings/116650.html Retrieved 08 07 2017

6.2 Pushing and Pulling, the Carrot or the Stick

As we are all different, we will, for certain have different management styles.

There are some of us that are more motivational, urging our team on, showing the best example.

Some of you will be more into organisation, structure and discipline, reminding your workers what is expected of them, and keeping them aware of the consequences of not reaching standards and targets.

The other way to express this, is the concept of the carrot and the stick.

The carrot is the promise of something positive, something worthwhile. What this might be; an all-expenses paid vacation for the best salesman, or a kind word or high praise from the manager, the good feelings are somewhere the same.

In the same fashion, the punishment for not fulfilling the wishes and demands of management, be they a; telling off, letter of warning, removal of a privilege, or what-ever, they clearly give the message that someone, somewhere, is not such a good feeling.

However, what should be always be kept in mind, that it is only reasonable to not push or pull them too much or too far.

If you think of the image of physically pulling or pushing someone. To a certain degree, intensity, this will help the person move forward.

Only, if the force, in either direction is too strong, then the person, sooner or later will lose their balance, and either stop, or fall down.

Neither of these two possibilities should be what you are looking for.

So, push or pull, by all means, but not too much.

And so, to your subordinates ….

6.3 The Shambling Sloth

The sloth is not a bad person, he is not even, at the base, a bad worker, he is just rather laid back in his attitude to the job.

More than likely he has been at this post quite a long time; knows the job forwards and backwards, and has seen generations of managers, come and go.

He surely knows every trick in the book of how not to do his job, and yet, not get fired for it.

He might also be a sort of expert in his area, so few people know enough to argue with him.

The first necessity is to be, to become or to bring in, an expert in this field, so that one can really, objectively assess his productivity.

Once you can prove to him that you know what, how much and how long each task should take, he will either shape up, or ship out.

6.4 Jim Head

When I was working as a trainee at Allied records, a record pressing factory. I had the good fortune to be under the direction of an excellent manager, Jim Head.

To understand this particular anecdote, you will need to first understand the process of creating vinyl disks, which is as follows:

The original disk is an object called an acetate, which is a soft material, cut into by a special recording needle.

The acetate is then electroplated with silver and then with a layer of nickel, this layer is then separated from the acetate, and is a reverse image of the side of the disk, this is called the father or master disk.

This master disk is then electroplated and that layer, when separated is termed, a mother disk. (The mother disk is a metal version of the final disk and can be played on a normal record player).

The mother is then electroplated to create the 'stampers', these stampers, (which have a relatively short life), are then placed on the pressing machines, into which the vinyl granules are poured, heated into a molten plastic, squirted in between the two stampers, and pressed into the form of a vinyl disk.

The creation of the master disk is a very highly specialised process, where-as, the making of the mother disks and the stampers, although specialised, is slightly less so.

The electroplating process uses a series of baths, in which the nickel solution is poured, the master or mother is rotated, using an electric current to attract the metal particles onto the disk.

The baths need to be kept pristine clean, and have to be emptied, cleaned and refilled on a regular basis.

It was this particular manoeuvre where the two young men that had worked in that department would mostly benefit from the technical ignorance of the plant manager.

They seriously informed their new manager, Jim Head, that this would take all of two days, and that there was nothing else that they could do during this time.

Unfortunately for them, Jim, although now working in management, was a university chemistry major. He turned to them and offered to do the whole cleaning operation, alone, in half a day.

They ran off, promising to do their best, and before the end of the day, that part of the process was back on line.

The sloth can and will work at almost the same speed as everyone else. Their laziness can also be a positive thing, for, trying to find a way to function using less effort, they could even end up as more efficient then your usual worker!

6.5 The Pandered Poodle

One of the most irritating personality traits that we might find in life is the feeling of 'entitlement'.

People that have this attitude towards life, can be most problematic because they expect to be very well treated, as a matter of course, whether, from the outside, they deserve it, or not.

There is the classic, 'daddy's girl', blonde, attractive, spoilt rotten.

Although they might just as well come from the opposite side of the rails, feeling that the poverty or sickness, (physical, mental or emotional) , experienced in their childhood, gives them some form of indelible right, to have more than everyone else, as a form of compensation.

I remember in my first year at university in Birmingham, I met a girl that was a friend of a friend.

We were shopping at Rackham's department store. She, without any shame, stole stuff, right in front of me. Her logic was that she was a poor student, while Rackham's was a rich store.

We find them in all walks of life, they are often the ones that know the rule books by heart.

Every right, obligation, salary structure and responsibility that the other; the enterprise, the armed services, might by statuted to undertake they know and insist on.

However, these people are not dishonest, only they have their own spin on what they deserve.

When I pointed out to my fellow student, that it wasn't Rackham's that was likely to suffer financially, because, to my knowledge, most big stores add a small percentage on the price of stuff to compensate for 'pilfering'.

And that it would be some poor, old age pensioner, that might really want something that was only available at that store who would be subsidising her light fingers.

At that point, she really stopped for a moment to reconsider her point of view.

As long as you take the time and the energy to fully listen and understand the expectations of these people, and then find a fair and reasonable response, they will react positively and invest in their tasks.

Unfortunately, we all know that life is not always fair, and we cannot always succeed to get our 'just rewards'.

In the case where your enterprise cannot or will not acquiesce to their justified demands, then your job is simply to inform the employee that these are the real working conditions of this job, today, and they are totally free to take this up with HR or upper management, or ultimately to leave. - The choice is entirely theirs.

In our group practice, we had exactly thus situation. The psychologists 'found out', that the amount of money billed for their work, came to about three times their take home salary. From this person's feeling of being unfairly treated they first reduced their billing hours, and then asked for a raise.

Our response was to explain why, with all the direct and indirect costs of our mini enterprise, it was not only usual but also necessary to have that one third, two thirds balance, but also to install a bonus system for those therapists who happened to bill over their usual quota.

Since that moment, everyone has worked correctly, but most of all, our pretty, pink, pampered, poodle.

6.6 Dory the blue-tang flatfish

She is sweet but possibly not firing on all pistons. How she has gotten this job, surely through some sort of personal contact with someone or a temporary job placement that no-one had the heart to end, but what is clear, she would never have passed a normal selection procedure.

So, you have inherited a semi functioning team member.

However, before you write someone like this off, just reflect on what she brings indirectly to the team.

These types of people often bring a sense of humanity to an office, and this kind of positive atmosphere is of great value and importance.

There are two categories of workers of this type; the very methodical and the scatterbrain.

The very methodical is likely to be the least intelligent, and yet, as long as they have repetitive tasks, that they can take their time to learn, they can be very helpful.

Just to be aware that they might have a limited capacity to realise if things are different and to adjust to new circumstances and situations.

The scatterbrain is more adaptive and more intelligent, here, what is necessary is that she reports to someone that is her direct supervisor, but not you. Someone that can delegate small specific tasks, and is close enough to the work to check that it is done as instructed.

One of the roles of a good manager is to be able to judge the strengths and weaknesses of all their subordinates, and to make the best use of their capacities.

6.7 The Cheeky Monkey

This is the impertinent, impolite, impudent colleague. He can be disrespectful, disruptive but often, terribly droll.

He is the office court jester, making fun and mockery of one and all.

But it is the 'one and all', where the problem lies. The implicit respect that he owes to you, due to your power and position doesn't seem to have registered for him.

Quite possibly you were work colleagues of similar status before you were promoted, or maybe he was a good pal of the last manager, who would allow this lack of managemental distance, as their understanding as to where to 'draw the line', was always totally clear, even if possibly only tacitly understood.

The other possibility is that your own personal style is slightly self-demeaning. This means that you positively attract people that will joke with and at you.

The self-depreciating attitude is something that I know all too well, as it is one of my own personality traits.

The trick in all of this, is, as in the advices in the book, linked to your own 'centre'. To be able to handle these types of people or situation, you need to be clear in who you are and what your position is.

You have to able judge just how far to let the other go, and at what point that you need to say, stop.

The less self-confidence that you have, the less you can let anyone get away with any form of disrespect.

Once you realise that you are the boss, and when you choose to draw the line, then the others are obliged to halt there, then you can allow quite a lot of leeway.

As a therapist, I have to deal with people that can have rather difficult personality traits.

In my own way of working, I choose to accept that the patients criticise me, if they feel that they have a legitimate grievance.

Borderline personality disorder, is one type of problematic where the person can easily feel abused, and can go very far in expressing it.

In one such situation, where the patient had been brought up with an abusive, denigrating father, I had done or not do something that he was not happy with.

So, I encouraged him to express his dissatisfaction. He started, and continued, and continued, I was beginning to feel particularly abused, myself.

I then turned, quietly to him and informed him that I had given him ample time and space to express his unhappiness, but now this was him abusing me, and now he must stop.

I was very quiet and clear.

He complained that he hadn't had enough time to say all that he wished to say.

I replied that for me, it was enough, and as it was my office, I had full right to decide what wasn't enough, and what was.

He tried several times to continue, but quietly and politely, I cut him off.

He stormed out of the room, slamming the door.

The next week he returned and thanked me. He had never been able to stop his father, once he got onto a subject. I had shown him how it could be done. It was a turning point in the therapy.

On a lighter note, I run a weekly group, now titled, 'Buried Treasure', with the theme, finding our hidden, inner resources. The group, (not surprisingly), is relaxed and laid back.

We have one or two 'jokers' in the group. Being a therapy group, I am quite severe about people not saying or doing anything to attack the other group members that might make them feel uncomfortable.

Being the group focaliser / animator, I have no such restriction, however, the banter goes both ways, and the participants have full permission to make remarks in my direction.

However, I still, from time to time, reign someone in, if I feel that they are going beyond my own comfort point, and there is a real lack of respect.

Allowing your subordinates a certain latitude to make fun of you is not a major fault, you and they must just be aware that you are the person that decides if and when this might be acceptable and just how far you will accept their banter.

There is a level of fun that helps in the relationship between you and your team, it just must never slide into the area of disrespect.

In our little group practice, my wife, as the psychiatrist, is the boss, however, I am the other founding partner and the administrator.

We run it, as much as possible in a very informal manner, and the psychologists that work for us treat us a little like a parental couple. However, as is my way, I still allow myself to be a bit the office clown, that the others have the right to make fun of – a bit. (Also, being the only man, and the oldest, this reduces a little the pressure).

So, to recap; allowing the office jester the liberty to sometimes jibe you, in the office, in front of the other office staff, is not a major problem.

Go with the punches, only be aware just how far you feel comfortable to go.

Never forgetting that you are the boss, and you decide when you feel that someone has reached the acceptable limit, and when to stop.

The openness to this sort of interaction can really help for the work atmosphere, people will find you more human and more approachable.

Hence, they should be able to come to you if they have any problems, trusting that you can hear their difficulties without immediately jumping on them as being at fault.

And even, when you do need to criticise or discipline someone, being seen as a humane manager, makes it much easier to accept and to improve, than having someone cold and aloof lecturing you.

6.8 The Sabre-toothed Shark

He will bite your bottom, trip you up, and, if at all possible, steal your job.

Yes, this is the dangerous one, and it is really important to identify him, as quickly as possible.

My father had an attitude when driving that is worth thinking on.

He was by no means a slow or timid driver, but, from time to time, when we were in a passing lane, we would find someone behind us, that wanted to go even faster than were going, even above the maximum speed limit, at which we were already driving.

My father would look for an opening in the traffic, even if it meant slowing down, so that the guy behind us would be able to pass.

"If someone wants to go faster than you wish to, move out of the way, and let them pass," was his reflection.

In this work situation, you will have one of three possible strategies:

Block him; check everything he is doing, every contact that he has or is making, destroy his work and reputation, ultimately get him moved or fired.

Go faster; work you ass off, suck up to upper management, make strategic alliances with the movers and shakers of your enterprise, take as much personal credit for the work of all your team. (Yes, I might be exaggerating a bit, but you get the general idea.)

Or, you could move out of the way; let him know that you can see how he wants to progress and offer to support him, as much as you are able. (Hopefully, he will respond positively, and not use your openness to stab you in the back.)

There is a fourth alternative, that is a combination of two and three; make a pact with him to push you both, higher and higher in the organisation.

As long as you are true to your word, validating for his work, all the while, doing what is necessary for you to continue to advance, you might become the dream team.

The main problem, as with all relationships, especially in an environment where someone is aiming to win something, it can be horribly difficult to know just how far they are likely to go to achieve their goals.

Which is to say, just how trustworthy they can be.

My basic philosophy in life is; 'Trust in God, but tie up your camel'. It is supposed to come from ancient Greece, but is also one of the reported sayings of the Islamic prophet Muhammad.

Most of the understandings of this is; 'God helps those that help themselves', but it is not this sense of the phrase that I am referring to.

My own reading of this, which seems most in tune with that of Muhammad, is that it is right to trust, but you must also be realistic and take reasonable precautions.

Even if you do succeed to have a meaningful conversation with the 'Shark', and it seems that you have an understanding, it would still seem wise to keep a careful eye on him.

Just to confirm to yourself, from time to time, that he is not plotting some form of 'coup d'état'.

However, if you do not succeed to come to any understanding with him, as he denies any strong desire to advance, or refuses any mutual support that you might offer him, you need to prepare for war.

The first, and often best policy is transparency and communication. If you have a reasonable relationship with your, (new), boss go and talk to him and reflect that you have some concerns about your hyperactive subordinate.

That he has done nothing wrong, but you have some concerns that his desire to advance might attract him to acting in ways that might be detrimental to your boss's department.

If you can have your boss on your side, it is already an important protection.

You might also do well to have the same conversation with your HR department, if you have one.

The next thing to watch is that his work ethic, which is likely to be strong, does not give him access to higher management, even in different departments.

If it forces you to work more, it is a necessary sacrifice, and it will get you, 'brownie points', (being well regarded), with your superiors.

What is important is to not block his work, but to keep it under your direct control at all times.

By all means, give him credit for his work, but make it clear that as he is your subordinate, you are the coordinator and most often the originator of all his work.

The image of riding a hot, young, stallion, comes to mind. The horse will want to gallop, fine.

Take him to a place where he can gallop safely, (a race would also fit into that description), when you feel it is okay, you release him from your tight control.

And you let him run, but you are still on the saddle, you are still holding the reins, the bit is still between his teeth. He runs, he gallops, he triple gallops, but he stays under your control, you are always master of the situation.

Likewise, your employee will want to run, to gallop, to triple gallop, so let him. All you need to do is to assure yourself that you keep control of this situation, and allow him to carry you, up and across.

If you allow a horse to run, to express itself, to experience its speed, strength and power, and yet, use your position of authority to keep it safe and looked after, sooner or later, it will accept that you direct it, and the benefit is mutual.

If you support this guy to advance with his projects, all the while clearly showing him that you will not relinquish your position as boss, there is a strong possibility that he will realise that you are his ally and not his enemy.

Once that understanding is acquired, you will have successfully tamed your sabre-toothed shark.

7 Final Reflections

Am I proud to have written this book?

Yes and no.

No, because it is not very spiritual; it doesn't focus on how, as developing humans, we are finding the highest path towards interacting with our fellow 'men'.

And yet, yes; I feel that I am offering something positive and useful, so as to be able to cope with and confront real working life.

I would be most happy to hear your thoughts and reflections, as well as a review on Goodreads, Amazon, or on your own Blog sites.

Thank you for taking the title to read this.

Kindest regards,

Gary.

Other works

By

Gary Edward Gedall

Island of Serenity Book 1

The Island of Survival

Pierre-Alain James 'Faron' Ferguson is about to commit suicide, in his suicide note he attempts to understand how he has come to have wrecked not only his own life, but also all of those around him.

Pierre-Alain James 'Faron' Ferguson finds himself in a type of 'no-mans-land', between here and there, he must accept to visit the 7 islands before he will be allowed to continue on to his next steps. The islands are named; Survival, Pleasure, Esteem, Love, Expression, Insight and lastly, the Island of Serenity

The Early Years:

Pierre-Alain James 'Faron' Ferguson is born into a well-to-do household of a factory owner, Scottish father and mother of a noble French family

He, and his younger brother Jay, grow up in a home of two distant but invested parents. Already, the first, small stones of his future problems are being put into place.

The Island of Survival:

Faron finds himself on the first of the seven islands, transformed into a prehistoric human form, he must learn how to interact with the local environment and the early humanoid tribe.

Here, he must reconnect with his instinct of survival.

Island of Serenity Book 2

Sun & Rain

This is the second chapter of Faron's life history, in which he falls in love, becomes a real cowboy, starts boarding school, finds his two best friends, goes to visit his weird aunt, goes skiing in Switzerland, and continues the relationship that brings him the greatest joy, yet the greatest sorrow in all of his life, but more than that would be telling too much.

FREE: If you have not yet read Book 1, Survival, no worries, I have included a shortened version, so as to introduce you to the story and the main characters.

Island of Serenity Book 3

The Island of Pleasure

Vol 1 Venice

Part 1.

Faron finds himself in a past version of Venice, as the owner of an old but grand hotel that doubles as the meeting place for the wealthy men of the City and the high-class escort girls that live in the establishment.

Faron can do anything that he likes without limitation or cost. Not only can he avail himself of the girls, but can eat and drink, without limit, but never suffer from a hangover, nor gain a gram.

So why has the enigmatic guide brought him here, and will his limitless access to life's offerings really bring him the pleasure that he is destined to experience?

Part 2.

Faron is transformed into an adolescent tom boy. In this more modern version of Venice, 'he' has just 7 days to be made into a high-class escort girl.

What does this experience and the intrigues of the other persons within his sphere, mean for him, on his continuing quest to understand, and to experience, Pleasure?

Island of Serenity Book 4

The Island of Pleasure

Vol 2 Japan

Faron finds himself in the mystery of a long-ago Japan, in the body of a young, trainee Geisha.

Who is this sad, young man that he must help to find back his pleasure in life?

Why must he hide the identity of his mother, from the rest of the world?

Why was the love of his mother's life, stolen away by her sister, known to all as Madame Butterfly?

What part does the feudal lord of the region have in all this?

And how does Faron finally succeed to find the key to rediscovering pleasure in his life?

Island of Serenity Book 5

Rise and Fall

In this the 5th book of the series, we watch as Faron grows from an adolescent into a young, driven man.

He begins by escaping to New York, before starting his University career, finding back his two school, best friends, Duncan and Mike.

After graduating, the three find themselves setting up a business, manufacturing, buying and importing goods from Indonesia.

Success seems to be just around the corner, but Faron cannot help himself. Bitterness and betrayal, hound him like a hungry dog.

To destroy, his own best friend, is not an act to take lightly, but take it, he does.

And what of Angelique, and his daughter Aideen? He is still emotionally entangled, but is that a good thing, or a very bad thing?

Only time will tell.

Island of Serenity Book 6

The Island of Esteem pt1

The Knight's Tale

Faron, our anti-hero, finds himself transported into the body of Sir Lancelot, in the continuation of this inspirational, fantasy series.

He is on the quest to heal his self-esteem, but the knight, although noble and brave, is also a flawed human-being. He avoids emotional conflicts, but cannot escape his passion for Guinevere.

Follow Lancelot through his tortured romantic journey, in a world of court intrigue, magic and heroism.

Island of Serenity Book 7

The Island of Esteem pt2

'Le Morte D'Arthur

In this second and concluding volume of the Island of Esteem, we follow Al, as he makes the transition from a hesitant and nervous teenager, to a self-assured and confident, young man.

Lancelot still is troubled by his past and present inability to impose himself, in any situation other than battle.

We then get to understand how it was that Lancelot was forgiven by Guinevere, and why Arthur accepted to call on his help to retrieve the Uffington sceptre. And how and why Al, chose and succeeded to steal it.

Finally, what happens after, to Lancelot, Arthur, …and Al.

Adventures with the Master

Dhargey was a sickly child or so his parents treated him. He was too weak to join the army or work in the fields or even join the monastery as a normal trainee monk.

To explain to the 'Young Master' why he should be accepted into the order with a lightened program, he was forced to accompany the revered old man a little way up the mountain.

As his parents watched him leave; somewhere they felt that they would never see their sickly, fragile boy ever again, somewhere they were totally right.

He was a happy, healthy seven year old until he witnessed the riders, dressed in red and black, destroying his village and murdering his parents; the trauma cut deep into his psyche.

Only the chance meeting with a wandering monk could set him back onto the road towards health and serenity.

Through meditation, initiations, stories, taming wild horses, becoming a monkey, mastering the staff and the sword; the future 'Young Master' prepares to face his greatest demon.

Two men, two journeys, one goal.

The Tales of Peter the Pixie

Peter the innocent, honest, young pixie, and his friends; Elli, the, 'much older then she looks', modest but powerful Fairy, Timothy, the old, trustworthy, Toad and the, ever so noble, Fire Dragon, are the best of friends.

Together, they experience many wonderful and heart-warming adventures.

Told in a classical children's story style; Peter and his friends, meet all kinds of creatures and situations.

As with all children, Peter is often confronted with experiences that he does not know how best to deal with, and he often reacts in ways that are not the most appropriate. Fortunately; with the help of his good friends, good will and common sense, everything always turns out for the best.

None Fiction:

The Zen Approach to Modern Living Vol 1

Fundamentals, Family & Friends

Life is often experienced as a series of conflicts and aggressions, both from the outside and within ourselves.

The Zen Approach to Modern Living series, will lead you towards a more harmonious way of dealing with the many, complex and competing elements of your daily life.

These conflicts leave us exhausted, depressed, angry, and feeling generally unhappy and unfulfilled.

Being more in harmony with yourself will bring more happiness, more energy and open up the route to self-fulfillment.

Volume 1 covers; an introduction to the basic concepts, our relationship with ourselves, our family, (partner, children, parents, brothers, sisters and in-laws), friends and enemies.

Plus, plus, plus, A Bonus Chapter: My Deepest, Darkest, Secret.

The Zen approach to Low Impact Training and Sports

A simple method for achieving a healthy body and a healthy mind

Many of us approach our fitness and sports activities in an aggressive and competitive fashion.

And even if we feel that we succeed to break out of our comfort zones and win against ourselves or our opponent, there is an important cost to bear.

This level of violence that we have come to accept, so as to reach our goals is also an aggression against ourselves. By removing this need to 'win at any price', and tuning in with our bodies and emotions, we can achieve an enormous amount, all the while being in harmony with our mind, body and spirit.

The Zen approach to Low Impact Training and Sports, is a new softer approach where you can have the best of all worlds.

REMEMBER
Stories and poems for self-help and self-development
based on techniques of Ericksonian and auto-hypnosis

Dusk falls, the world shrinks little by little into a smaller and smaller circle as the light continues to diminish.

The centre of this world is illuminated by a small, crackling sun; the flames dance, and the rough faces of the people gathered there are lit by the fire of their expectations.

The old man will begin to speak, he will explain to them how the world is, how it was, how it was created. He will help them understand how things have a sense, an order, a way that they need to be.

He will clarify the sources of un-wellness and unhappiness, what is sickness, where it comes from, how to notice it and... how to heal it.

To heal the sick, he will call forth the forces of the invisible realms, maybe he will sing, certainly he will talk, and talk, and talk.

Since the beginning of time we have gathered round those who can bring us the answers to our questions and the means to alleviate our sufferings.

This practice has not fundamentally changed since the earliest times; in every era, continent and culture we have found and continue to find these experiences.

In this, amongst the oldest of the healing traditions, he has succeeded to meld modern therapy theories and techniques with stories and poems of the highest quality.

With much humanity, clinical vignettes, common sense and lots of humour, the reader is gently carried from situation to situation. Whether the problems described concern you directly, indirectly or not at all, you will surely find interest and benefits from the wealth of insights and advices contained within and the conscious or unconscious positive changes through reading the stories and poems.

Picturing the Mind   Vol 1

A simple model capable to explain the functioning and dysfunctioning of the human psyche.

Introduction to the Field theory of Human Functioning

For the average man and woman in the street, the complex and competing theories and models of the human psyche; its development, functioning and dis-functioning are often unhelpful for their understanding of themselves.
This becomes even more problematic when they find themselves in difficulty, as often, even the mental health professionals, who are experts in their own fields, find themselves at a loss to communicate successfully how and why the patent is unwell and what needs to happen to find or regain a healthy balance.

This opens up the question; 'is it possible to image a simple, single model, accessible to everyone, to explain the development, functioning and dis-functioning of the human psyche?'

One that builds on existing theories and models, benefitting from the mass of experience and research of 'modern western' psychological concepts and ideas, but also integrating traditional visions of the human psyche and modern theories from the physical sciences.

Picturing the Mind, is an attempt to answer to this need.

Picturing the Mind Vol 2

The second volume following on from the initial concepts will reflect on such subjects as:

Relationships

Exchanging energy

Heart & Soul

Recuperation

Subjective constructions

An unconscious yes, an unconscious no

Me, myself and everyone else

Circles in circles, the micro level

Circles in circles, the macro level

Intuition

Metaphysical reflections

Picturing the Mind

Vol 3

Will deal with:

Psychopathology

Traditional psychotherapy

&

Alternative therapeutic approaches.

www.ingramcontent.com/pod-product-compliance
Lightning Source LLC
Chambersburg PA
CBHW051534020426
42333CB00016B/1924